Assessing Key Objectives in Numeracy

LEN AND ANNE FROBISHER

2

Linacre House, Jordan Hill, Oxford, OX2 8DP
a division of Reed Educational and Professional Publishing Ltd
www.ginn.co.uk

Ginn is a registered trademark of Reed Educational and Professional Publishing Ltd

ISBN 0 602 29705 2

05 04 03 02 01
10 9 8 7 6 5 4 3 2 1

Typeset by Artistix, Thame, Oxon
Illustrated by Stephanie Strickland
Printed and bound in Great Britain by Ashford Colour Press, Gosport, Hants

Contents

Year 2 key objective	Oral assessment	Written assessments
1 Count, read, write and order whole numbers to at least 100; know what each digit represents (including 0 as a place holder).	6	19
2 Describe and extend simple number sequences (including odd/even numbers, counting on or back in ones or tens from any 2-digit number, and so on).	7	23
3 Understand that subtraction is the inverse of addition; state the subtraction corresponding to a given addition and vice versa.	8	27
4 Know by heart all addition and subtraction facts for each number to at least 10.	9	31
5 Use knowledge that addition can be done in any order to do mental calculations more efficiently.	10	35
6 Understand the operation of multiplication as repeated addition or as describing an array.	11	39
7 Know and use halving as the inverse of doubling.	12	43
8 Know by heart facts for the 2 and 10 multiplication tables.	13	47
9 Estimate, measure and compare lengths, masses and capacities, using standard units; suggest suitable units and equipment for such measurements.	14	51
10 Read a simple scale to the nearest labelled division, including using a ruler to draw and measure lines to the nearest centimetre.	15	53
11 Use the mathematical names for common 2D and 3D shapes; sort shapes and describe some of their features.	16	59
12 Use mathematical vocabulary to describe position, direction and movement.	17	63
13 Choose and use appropriate operations and efficient calculation strategies to solve problems, explaining how the problem was solved.	18	67

Introduction

Assessing Key Objectives is an effective and straightforward resource for medium- and long-term assessment of key objectives from the National Numeracy Strategy *Framework for teaching mathematics from Reception to Year 6*. The series comprises seven books, one for each of Reception to Year 6, providing teachers with material with which to review and record children's progress.

This book contains:

- thirteen oral (medium-term) assessments, one for each key objective
- thirteen written (medium-term) assessments
- a Getting ready (long-term) assessment, covering the whole curriculum including the key objectives, and designed to be given before the National Curriculum Tests.

Children's responses to the assessment tasks will provide you with valuable insights into their progress, understanding and thinking in relation to each key objective.

Oral assessments

Each oral assessment is a simple means of assessing one key objective and can be completed in a very short time. It is intended that the assessments be used with children individually or in small groups, either on completion of the teaching of the key objective, or at the end of the half term in which the teaching has been completed.

The assessments consist of practical activities with readily available materials, and involve children working mentally and responding mainly orally. There are three parts to each assessment with each part targeting a different aspect of the key objective.

Each assessment indicates possible equipment; this is only a suggestion, as similar materials may be readily available in the classroom and satisfy the same purpose.

Also given are suggested questions to ask. These must be viewed as only suggestions and should be replaced, where appropriate, by similar questions using language with which children are familiar.

Written assessments

The written assessments are in the form of three tests (A, B and C) to be used with a whole class or small groups. Each set of three tests targets one key objective. You may wish to help children read some questions so that the language does not prevent them from answering.

Written assessment A is a one-page test which aims to assess the very early teaching and easier aspects of a key objective. This may be used formatively, providing feedback for future lessons, and can also be used with low achievers at the end of the teaching of the key objective in order to provide them with questions that they are able to complete.

Written assessment B is a two-page test. It aims to assess a wide range of ideas in a key objective and is suitable for the majority of a class. Like Written assessment A, it can be used formatively as a means of determining what children know and do not know in relation to a key objective, leading to remediation where appropriate. It can also be used as a summative assessment, providing an indication of children's performance and contributing to their records in mathematics for the year.

Written assessment C is a one-page test designed for those children who show particular aptitude in a key objective by scoring highly on Written assessment B. The questions are more challenging and demanding, often requiring children to connect and use an aspect of the key objective with ideas found in other key objectives.

Getting ready assessment

The Getting ready assessment is designed to provide children with practice questions similar to those they are likely to meet in the National Curriculum (NC) Test and should be given to children towards the end of the spring term. This will enable teachers to see which aspects of the curriculum need to be looked at early in the summer term to prepare for the NC Test.

The Getting ready assessment is designed to allow flexibility in long-term assessment. You may wish to assess children only in relation to the key objectives, or to assess children's performance across the whole of the mathematics curriculum. The Getting ready assessment is therefore divided into two parts:

- Part A targets the key objectives
- Part B covers the remaining objectives.

You may prefer to give both Part A and Part B of the Getting ready assessment to the children in small chunks, for example three or four pages at at time. Again, help children to read the questions where necessary.

Recording

Three record sheets are provided:
- the Individual record sheet
- the Class record sheet
- the National Curriculum Levels record sheet.

The Individual record sheet is intended to be photocopied for each child. It lists each of the key objectives and enables you to record results of oral assessments and each of the written assessments as appropriate.

Space is also provided for supplementary notes if the child's progress in any key objective differs markedly from that of the rest of the class.

A column labelled 'code' is also provided for each assessment. This may be used to record, either by letter, number or colour code:

- A: if a child has met the key objective in full
- B: if the key objective needs more attention, having been met only partially
- C: if the child has had very little success in meeting the key objective
- N: if the key objective has not been covered in previous teaching.

The Class record sheet lists the key objectives and can be used to summarize the performance of all the children. It gives an overall picture of how the class as a whole has performed on the Written assessment for each key objective. You may wish to use the same coding as suggested for the Individual record sheet.

It can also be used to record children's performance on Parts A and B of the Getting ready assessment, which could then be passed to the Year 3 teacher, together with the Individual record sheets.

The National Curriculum Levels record sheet enables teachers:

- to record the numerical (raw) score that each child achieves on the Getting ready assessment
- to record the score as a percentage, giving an approximate National Curriculum Level.

The example below shows how the score of 131 out of 229 for Jason Harper has been recorded as 57%, indicating a Level 2.

	Name	Raw score	Working towards Level 1			Level 1			Level 2			Level 3	Level 4
			\multicolumn{10}{c	}{Percentage score}									
			0	10	20	30	40	50	60	70	80	90	100
1	Jason Harper	131							✗				

Oral assessment 1

Key objective: Count, read, write and order whole numbers to at least 100; know what each digit represents (including 0 as a place holder).

Equipment: at least 50 cubes, set of 0–9 number cards, number cards 9, 28, 44, 70 and 82

Assessment a

Put out the cubes.

Count out 36 cubes for me.
Group your cubes into twos.
Check how many cubes you have by counting in twos.

Group your cubes into fives.
Check how many cubes you have by counting in fives.

Group your cubes into tens.
Check how many cubes you have by counting in tens.

Assessment b

Put out the 0–9 number cards.

| 0 | 1 | 2 | 3 | 4 | 5 | 6 | 7 | 8 | 9 |

Use the number cards to make the number 57.

| 5 | 7 |

What number have I made?
What does the 5 digit represent?

Use the number cards to make the number 80.

| 8 | 0 |

What does the 0 digit represent in the number 80?
Show me how to write the number 80 in words.

Assessment c

Draw these five boxes on paper:

| | 38 | | 61 | |

Write numbers in the three empty boxes so that the five numbers are in order.

Put out randomly the five number cards:

| 28 | 82 | 44 | 9 | 70 |

Tell me what these numbers are.
Put them in order, largest first.
How did you decide that 82 was more than 70?
How did you decide that 9 was less than 28?

Key objective: Describe and extend simple number sequences (including odd/even numbers, counting on or back in ones or tens from any 2-digit number, and so on).

Equipment: 1–100 square, set of 1–30 number cards

Assessment a

Start at 18. Count on in ones to 40.
Count on 5 from 77. What number did you end at?
Count on from 42 to 46. How many did you count?

Start at 73. Count back in ones to 50.
Count back 4 from 31. What number did you end at?
Count back from 67 to 62. How many did you count?

Assessment b

You may wish to let the child use a 1–100 square.

Start at 23. Count on in tens to 73.
Count on 50 in tens from 20.
What number did you end at?
Count on in tens from 40 to 90.
How many tens did you count?

Start at 65. Count back in tens to 15.
Count back 30 in tens from 80.
What number did you end at?
Count back in tens from 70 to 20.
How many tens did you count?

1	2	3	4	5	6	7	8	9	10
11	12	13	14	15	16	17	18	19	20
21	22	23	24	25	26	27	28	29	30
31	32	33	34	35	36	37	38	39	40
41	42	43	44	45	46	47	48	49	50
51	52	53	54	55	56	57	58	59	60
61	62	63	64	65	66	67	68	69	70
71	72	73	74	75	76	77	78	79	80
81	82	83	84	85	86	87	88	89	90
91	92	93	94	95	96	97	98	99	100

Assessment c

Spread the 1–30 number cards randomly face down on the table.

Turn over a card. What is the number?
Is it an even number or an odd number?
How did you decide?

Repeat the activity with other cards.

Key objective: Understand that subtraction is the inverse of addition; state the subtraction corresponding to a given addition and vice versa.

Equipment: cubes, set of 1–9 number cards

Assessment a

Put out the cubes.

Count out seven cubes for yourself.
Here are five more cubes for you. How many cubes do you have now?
If I took away five of your cubes, how many would you have left?

Count out ten cubes for yourself.
Give me three of your cubes. How many cubes do you have now?
If I gave you back your three cubes, how many cubes would you have?

Assessment b

On paper write the addition 7 + 9 = 16.

Tell me what this says.
Write me a subtraction that uses the same three numbers (7, 9 and 16).
Tell me how you decided what to do.

On paper write the subtraction 11 − 3 = 8.

Tell me what it says.
Write me an addition that uses the same three numbers (11, 3 and 8).
Tell me how you decided what to do.

Assessment c

Put out the 1–9 number cards.

Choose three of these numbers to make an addition with one of the numbers as an answer.
Make another addition with the same three numbers.
Make a subtraction with the same three numbers.
Make another subtraction with the same three numbers.

Key objective: Know by heart all addition and subtraction facts for each number to at least 10.

Equipment: two sets of 0–10 number cards, operation cards + and –, = card, two blank cards

Assessment a

What is 3 add 2? Add 1 to 4.
How many is 2 plus 6? What is the sum of 5 and 3?
What do you add to 7 to make 9?

Use the number cards to set out the open addition:

Use your number cards to make as many pairs of numbers as you can that add up to 6.

Set out the open addition:

Use your number cards to make as many additions to 3 as you can.

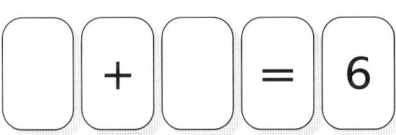

Assessment b

What is 4 take away 1? Take 3 from 5.
How many is 7 subtract 2? What is 6 less than 9?
How many more is 8 than 5?

Use the number cards to set out the open subtraction:

Use your number cards to make as many subtractions as you can that have the answer 4.

Set out the open subtraction:

Use your number cards to make as many subtractions from 5 as you can.

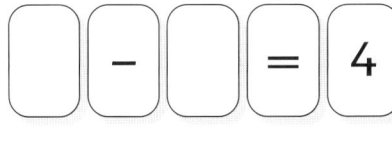
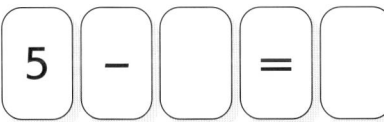

Assessment c

What is 9 add 2? Take 4 from 11. Add 5 to 7.
How many is 12 take away 6?
How many more than 8 is 13?
How many less than 14 is 9?

Tell me some additions that have 15 as the answer.
Tell me some subtractions that have 10 as the answer.

Key objective: Use knowledge that addition can be done in any order to do mental calculations more efficiently.

Equipment: set of 1–30 number cards, set of 30–90 multiple-of-ten cards, operation card +, = card

Assessment a

Put out each addition before asking the question.

What is 19 add 2?
Tell me how you did it.

How many is 4 add 28?
Tell me how you did it.

Add 70 to 20.
Tell me how you did it.

| 19 | + | 2 | = |

| 4 | + | 28 | = |

| 20 | + | 70 | = |

Assessment b

Put out each set of numbers before asking the question.

What is the sum of 8, 2 and 7?
Tell me how you did it.

What is the sum of 8, 7 and 2?
Tell me how you did it.

Find the total of 6, 8 and 4.
Tell me how you did it.

Check your answer by finding the total of 6, 8 and 4 in a different way. Tell me how you did it.

| 8 | 2 | 7 |

| 8 | 7 | 2 |

| 6 | 8 | 4 |

Assessment c

Put out each addition before asking the question.

Add 15 to 13.
Tell me how you did it.

What is 26 add 12?
Tell me how you did it.

Find a pair of numbers, both more than 10, that add up to 26.
Tell me how you did it.

Find another pair of numbers, both more than 10, that add up to 26.
Tell me how you did it.

| 13 | + | 15 | = |

| 26 | + | 12 | = |

Key objective: Understand the operation of multiplication as repeated addition or as describing an array.

Equipment: interlocking cubes

Assessment a

What is the answer to 4 add 4 add 4?
How did you do it?
How many is three lots of 4?
How did you do it?
Why is the answer to 4 add 4 add 4 the same as the answer to three lots of 4?

How many is 4 times 5?
How did you do it?
What is the answer to 5 add 5 add 5 add 5?
Why are the answers the same?

Assessment b

Put out some interlocking cubes.

Use six cubes to make a rectangle.
How many cubes in this row? (Point to the top row.)
Repeat for the other rows.

How many cubes in this column? (Point to the left-hand column.)
Repeat for the other columns.

How does the rectangle help you to find the answer to 2 times 3?
How does the rectangle help you to find the answer to 3 times 2?

or

Assessment c

Put out some interlocking cubes.

Make three sets with 6 cubes in each set.
How many cubes are there altogether?
How many is 6 add 6 add 6?
What is three lots of 6?

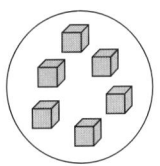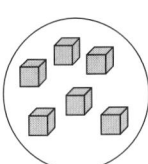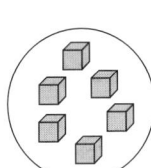

Make each set of six cubes into a six-stick.
Put the sticks together to make a rectangle.

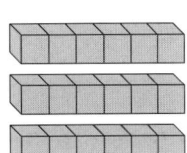

What multiplication does the rectangle show?
What is the answer to 3 times 6?

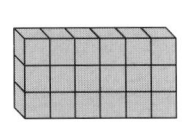 or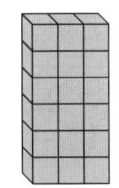

Key objective: Know and use halving as the inverse of doubling.

Equipment: interlocking cubes, a bag

Assessment a

Put out some cubes.

Count out three cubes for yourself.
Give me double the number of cubes you have.
How many cubes have you given me?
I am going to give you half of my cubes. How many will I give you?

I have some cubes in a bag.
I double the number of cubes in the bag. I then halve the number of cubes.
At the end I have 10 cubes.
How many cubes were in the bag to start with?
How did you work it out?

(You may wish to repeat this to help the child understand what is happening.)

Assessment b

Put out some cubes.

Count out eight cubes.
Give me half of your cubes.
How many cubes have you given me?
I am going to give you double the number that I have. How many will I give you?

I have some cubes in a bag.
I halve the number of cubes in the bag. I then double the number of cubes.
At the end I have 16 cubes.
How many cubes were in the bag to start with?
How did you work it out?

(You may wish to repeat this to help the child understand what is happening.)

Assessment c

I am going to tell you a calculation and then ask a question. Are you ready?
Double 14 is 28. How many is one-half of 28?
How did you work it out?

Here is another.
One-half of 38 is 19. How many is double 19?
How did you work it out?

Key objective: Know by heart facts for the 2 and 10 multiplication tables.

Equipment: sets of 2 times and 10 times table cards, sets of division by 2 and 10 cards without answers

Assessment a

Say your 2 times table for me.

What is 4 twos?
How many is 6 times 2?
Tell me the answer to 3 multiplied by 2.
Multiply 7 by 2.

Repeat for other numbers.

Assessment b

Say your 10 times table for me.

How many is 3 multiplied by 10?
Multiply 10 by 8.
What is 6 tens?
Tell me the answer to 9 times 10.

Repeat for other numbers.

Assessment c

I am going to tell you a calculation and then ask you a question. Are you ready?

Put out the multiplications and divisions as you say them.

2 times 10 is 20.
What is 20 divided by 2?
How did you work it out?

Here's another.
2 times 10 is 20.
What is 20 divided by 10?
How did you work it out?

How many twos in 20?
How many tens in 20?
Divide 20 by 2.
Divide 20 by 10.

$$2 \times 10 = 20$$

$$20 \div 2 =$$

$$2 \times 10 = 20$$

$$20 \div 10 =$$

(You may wish to assess children without using cards.)

Key objective: Estimate, measure and compare lengths, masses and capacities, using standard units; suggest suitable units and equipment for such measurements.

Equipment: a selection of measuring equipment, an apple, a bottle or container

Assessment a

Tell me a unit of measure that would be sensible for finding the length of the classroom. Which of these would you use to measure the length of the classroom? (Point to the equipment.)

How long do you think the classroom is?
Measure the length of the classroom to see if you are right.

Tell me something that is shorter than the length of the classroom.
Tell me something that is longer than the length of the classroom.

Assessment b

Put out an apple.

Tell me a unit of measure that would be sensible for finding the weight of the apple. Which of these would you use to measure the weight of the apple? (Point to the equipment.)

How much do you think the apple weighs?
Measure the weight of the apple to see if you are right.

Tell me something that is lighter than the apple.
Tell me something that is heavier than the apple.

Assessment c

Put out an empty bottle or container.

Tell me a unit of measure that would be sensible for finding how much this bottle will hold. Which of these would you use to measure how much it holds? (Point to the equipment.)

How much do you think the bottle holds?
Measure the capacity of the bottle to see if you are right.

Tell me something that holds more than the bottle.
Tell me something that holds less than the bottle.

Key objective: Read a simple scale to the nearest labelled division, including using a ruler to draw and measure lines to the nearest centimetre.

Equipment: ruler labelled in cm, scales labelled in 100 g, a measuring jug labelled in 200 mL, three objects to weigh, three containers

Assessment a

Have ready three straight lines measuring 8 cm, 5 cm and 10 cm drawn on paper, and a ruler.

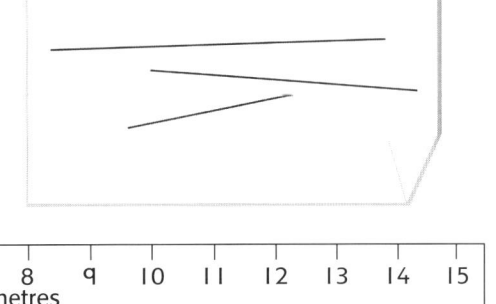

Without measuring, tell me which line you think is the longest/shortest.
Use the ruler to measure the length of each line.
How many centimetres is each line?

Draw across the page a line which is 16 cm long.
Draw down the page a line which is 7 cm long.
Draw a sloping line which is 12 cm long.

Assessment b

Put out three objects and a set of scales.

Without measuring, tell me which object you think is the heaviest/lightest.
How many grams do you think each object weighs?
Check your estimates using the scales.

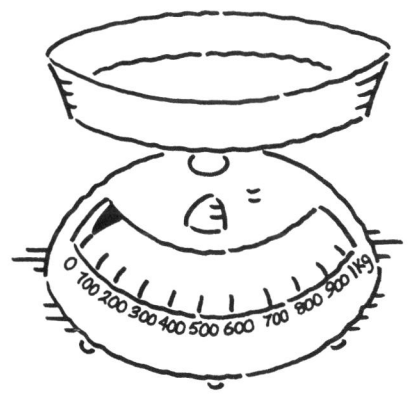

Assessment c

Put out three containers and the measuring jug.

Without measuring, tell me which container you think holds the most/least.
How much do you think each of the containers holds?
Check your estimates using the measuring jug.

Key objective: Use the mathematical names for common 2D and 3D shapes; sort shapes and describe some of their features.

Equipment: a selection of 2D and 3D shapes

Assessment a

Put out the 2D shapes.

Point to a hexagon.

What is this shape called?

Repeat with other shapes.

Mix up the shapes.

Point to the circle.

Repeat with other shapes.

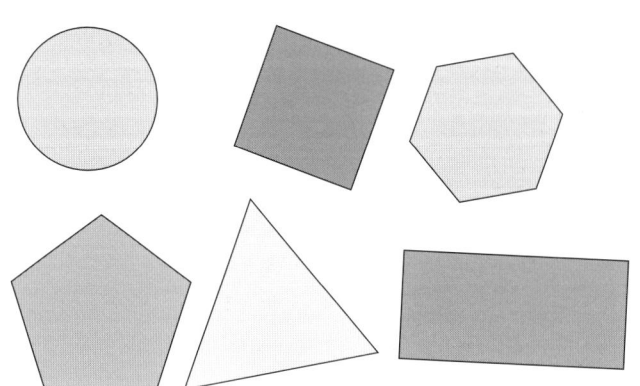

Assessment b

Put out the 3D shapes.

Point to a cube.

What is this shape called?

Repeat with other shapes.

Mix up the shapes.

Point to the pyramid.

Repeat with other shapes.

Point to the circular face on the cone.

What shape is this face?

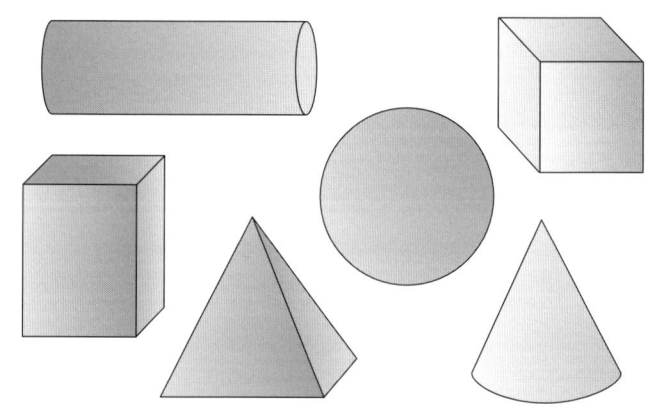

Assessment c

Put out the 3D shapes.

Sort these solids for me in any way you wish.
Tell me how you have sorted the solids.

Now sort them in a different way.
Tell me how you sorted them this time.

Repeat with the 2D shapes.

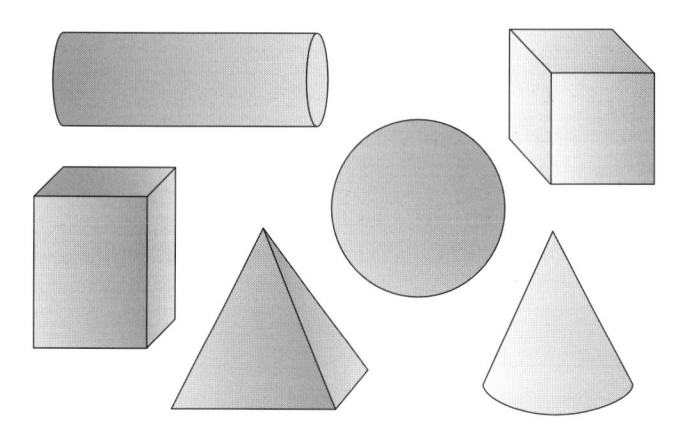

Key objective: Use mathematical vocabulary to describe position, direction and movement.

Equipment: cubes of different colours, 2 cm squared paper

Assessment a

Put out the cubes and the squared paper.

Place a red cube in the centre of the paper.
Place a green cube in a corner square of the paper.
Place a blue cube at one edge of the paper.
Place a yellow cube below the red cube.
Place an orange cube above the blue cube.
Place a brown cube between the red cube and the green cube.

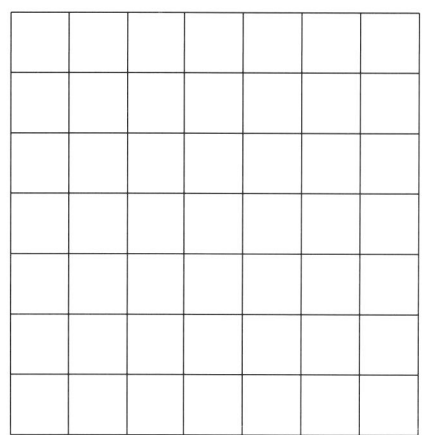

Assessment b

Put out the squared paper and place a cube in a square near the centre.

Move the cube two squares to your left.
Now move the cube three squares up.
Next move the cube five squares to your right.
Now move the cube four squares down.

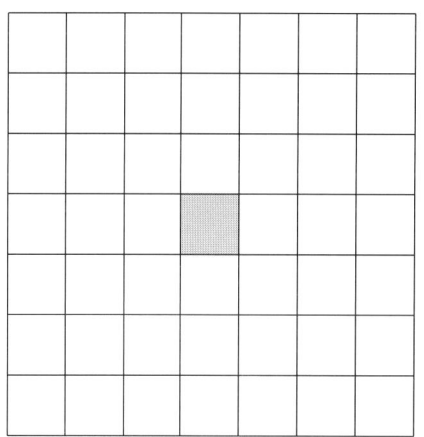

Assessment c

Ask the child to stand facing you.

Make a whole turn clockwise.
Now make a whole turn anticlockwise.
Make a half turn anticlockwise.
Turn clockwise through a right angle.
Make a quarter turn anticlockwise.

Key objective: Choose and use appropriate operations and efficient calculation strategies to solve problems, explaining how the problem was solved.

Assessment a

I am going to ask you a question. I want you to find the answer and then tell me how you did it. Are you ready?
9 take away 7.
How did you do it?

18 add 5.
How did you do it?

Add 23 to 41.
How did you do it?

Assessment b

I am going to tell you a calculation. I want you to make up a number story about the calculation. Are you ready?

11 add 12 makes 23. (Repeat the calculation.)
Now tell me a number story about this calculation.

Repeat with the following:

3 times 2 is 6.
8 subtract 5 equals 3.
10 divided by 2 is 5.

Assessment c

I am going to tell you a calculation, but instead of saying add, subtract, multiply or divide, I will say 'plop'. You have to tell me what 'plop' should be. Are you ready?

12 plop 9 is 3.
2 plop 4 equals 8.
20 plop 10 is 2.
7 plop 6 is 13.

Key objective: Count, read, write and order whole numbers to at least 100; know what each digit represents (including 0 as a place holder).

Name: **Date:**

1

How many tins on the shelves altogether? ☐

---

2 Match the numbers to their names.

32	60	14	23	41

sixty   thirty-two   forty-one   fourteen   twenty-three

---

3 Write the numbers in the box in order, **largest** first.

54	29	30	45	92

☐   ☐   ☐   ☐   ☐

---

4 Circle each number that has two tens.

Put a square around each number that has seven ones.

72   14   29   37   20   74

Key objective: Count, read, write and order whole numbers to at least 100; know what each digit represents (including 0 as a place holder).

Name: _____   Date: _____

1

How many geese? ☐

2 Each pack has two cartons of orange drink.

How many cartons? ☐

3 Asif makes his cubes into sticks of ten.

How many cubes has Asif? ☐

4 Write the missing numbers and number names.

| 19 | ☐ | 94 | ☐ |

↕   ↕   ↕   ↕

....   forty-three   ....   eighty

5 Write the numbers in the box in order, smallest first.

| 21 | 7 | 78 |
| 87 | 50 | 12 |

◻ ◻ ◻ ◻ ◻ ◻

6 Write the numbers in figures.

three tens and eight ones ⟶ ◻   five ones ⟶ ◻

seven ones and two tens ⟶ ◻   six tens ⟶ ◻

7 Write where the numbers 30, 80 and 50 go on the 0 to 100 number line.

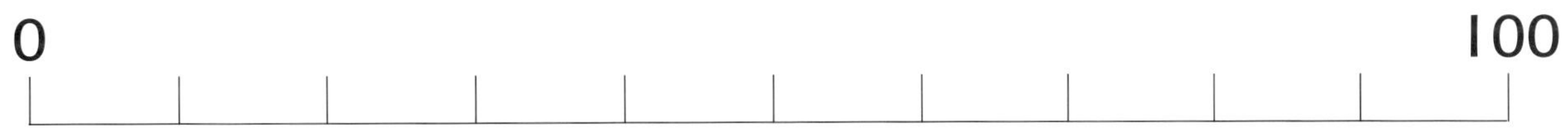

0   100

8 Write in the missing numbers.

54 ⟶ ◻ tens and ◻ ones

80 ⟶ ◻ tens and ◻ ones

7 ⟶ ◻ tens and ◻ ones

61 ⟶ ◻ tens and ◻ one

Key objective: Count, read, write and order whole numbers to at least 100; know what each digit represents (including 0 as a place holder).

Name: Date:

1

Each packet has 10 biscuits.

How many biscuits are there altogether? ☐

2   This is part of a 1 to 100 square.

Write in the missing numbers.

	87
96	

3   **a**   Use the digits ②, ④ and ⑦ to make five more tens and units numbers.

☐4☐7☐   ☐☐   ☐☐

☐☐   ☐☐   ☐☐

b   Which number has two ones and seven tens? ☐

c   Write five of the numbers in order, largest first.

☐☐   ☐☐   ☐☐   ☐☐   ☐☐

Key objective: Describe and extend simple number sequences (including odd/even numbers, counting on or back in ones or tens from any 2-digit number, and so on).

Name: **Date:**

1   Write the missing numbers in the number track, counting on in ones.

13	14	15						

2   Write the missing numbers in the number track, counting back in ones.

27	26	25						

3   Write the missing numbers in the number track, counting on in tens.

11	21	31						

4   Write the missing numbers in the number track, counting back in tens.

86	76	66						

5   Circle each even number in this grid.

1	2	3	4	5
6	7	8	9	10
11	12	13	14	15

Key objective: Describe and extend simple number sequences (including odd/even numbers, counting on or back in ones or tens from any 2-digit number, and so on).

Name: **Date:**

1 Write the missing numbers in the number track, counting on in ones.

			45	46	47				

2 Write the missing numbers in the number track, counting back in ones.

			58	57	56				

3 Write the missing numbers in the number track, counting on in tens.

			33	43	53				

4 Write the missing numbers in the number track, counting back in tens.

			66	56	46				

5 Circle the odd numbers.

7   12   18   23   30   35   40

6 Circle the even numbers.

5   10   19   24   30   32   37

7 **a** Count on seven from 45.

What number did you end on? ☐

b Count back six from 32.

What number did you end on? ☐

c Count on from 51 to 55.

How many did you count? ☐

d Count back from 78 to 73.

How many did you count? ☐

---

8 **a** Count on three tens from 24.

What number did you end on? ☐

b Count back four tens from 65.

What number did you end on? ☐

c Count on in tens from 33 to 73.

How many tens did you count? ☐

d Count back in tens from 88 to 58.

How many tens did you count? ☐

Key objective: Describe and extend simple number sequences (including odd/even numbers, counting on or back in ones or tens from any 2-digit number, and so on).

Name: **Date:**

1   Write in the missing numbers.

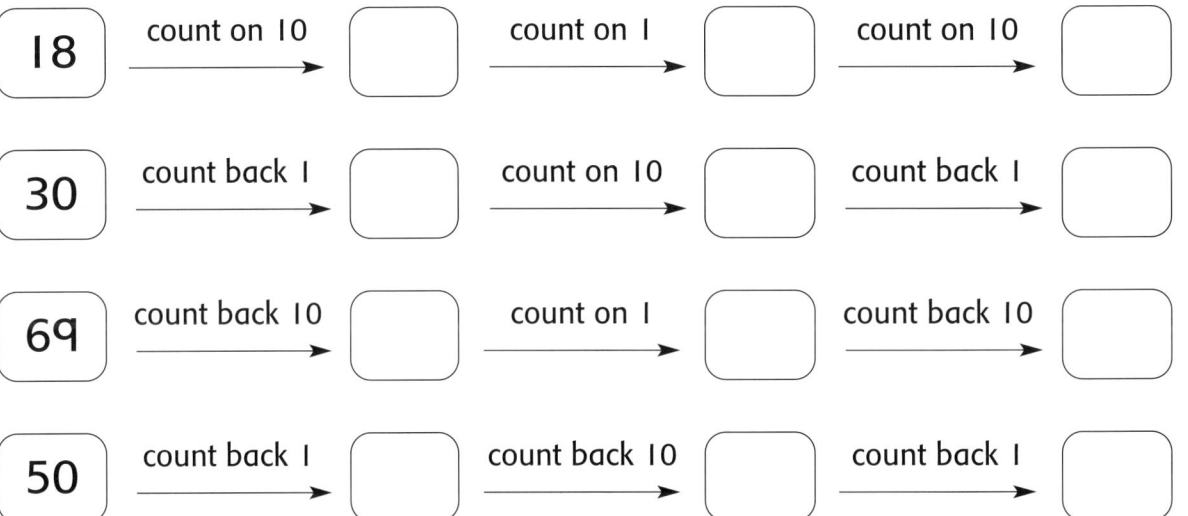

2   Sort the numbers in the box on the sorting grid.

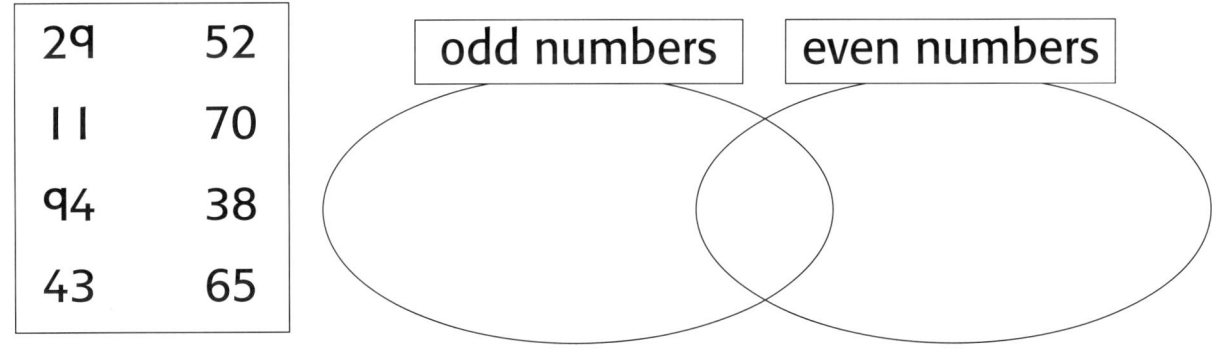

29	52
11	70
94	38
43	65

3   Write the next three numbers in each sequence.

a   26   36   46   56

b   39   37   35   33

c   16   18   20   22

Key objective: Understand that subtraction is the inverse of addition; state the subtraction corresponding to a given addition and vice versa.

Name: **Date:**

1 Write in the missing numbers.

a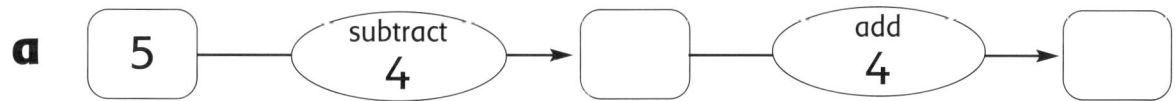

b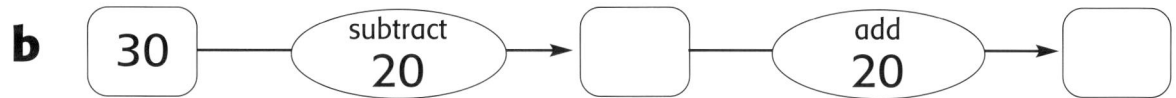

c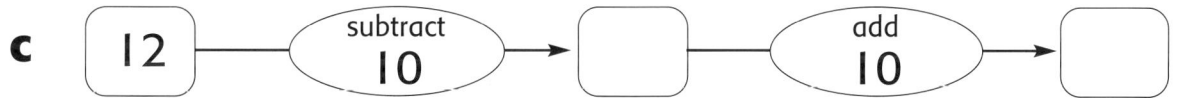

2 Write in the missing numbers.

a

b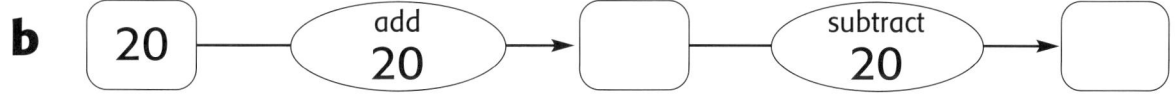

c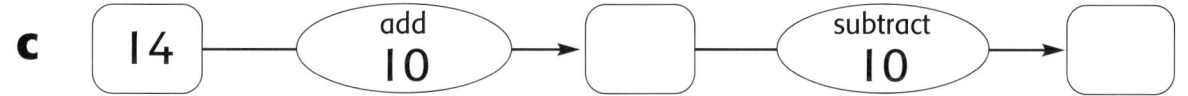

3 Write a subtraction that corresponds to the addition.

a $3 + 2 = 5$ ⟶ ☐ − ☐ = ☐

b $10 + 30 = 40$ ⟶ ☐ − ☐ = ☐

4 Write an addition that corresponds to the subtraction.

a $6 - 2 = 4$ ⟶ ☐ + ☐ = ☐

b $30 - 10 = 20$ ⟶ ☐ + ☐ = ☐

Key objective: Understand that subtraction is the inverse of addition; state the subtraction corresponding to a given addition and vice versa.

Name: **Date:**

I Write in the missing numbers.

a [6]——(+ 16)——▸[ ]——(– 16)——▸[ ]

b [50]——(+ 40)——▸[ ]——(– 40)——▸[ ]

c [35]——(+ 10)——▸[ ]——(– 10)——▸[ ]

d Why is the last number always the same as the first number?

....

....

2 Write in the missing numbers.

a [17]——(– 5)——▸[ ]——(+ 5)——▸[ ]

b [70]——(– 30)——▸[ ]——(+ 30)——▸[ ]

c [49]——(– 10)——▸[ ]——(+ 10)——▸[ ]

d Why is the last number always the same as the first number?

....

....

3 Write a subtraction that corresponds to the addition.

   a $8 + 17 = 25 \longrightarrow \boxed{} - \boxed{} = \boxed{}$

   b $50 + 30 = 80 \longrightarrow \boxed{} - \boxed{} = \boxed{}$

4 Write an addition that corresponds to the subtraction.

   a $19 - 6 = 13 \longrightarrow \boxed{} + \boxed{} = \boxed{}$

   b $70 - 20 = 50 \longrightarrow \boxed{} + \boxed{} = \boxed{}$

5 **a** $42 + 7 - 7 = \boxed{}$ **b** $20 + 33 - 33 = \boxed{}$

   c $32 + 14 - 14 = \boxed{}$ **d** $30 + 50 - 50 = \boxed{}$

   e $55 + 20 - 20 = \boxed{}$ **f** $400 + 200 - 200 = \boxed{}$

6 **a** $95 - 3 + 3 = \boxed{}$ **b** $60 - 9 + 9 = \boxed{}$

   c $36 - 11 + 11 = \boxed{}$ **d** $54 - 10 + 10 = \boxed{}$

   e $80 - 30 + 30 = \boxed{}$ **f** $600 - 300 + 300 = \boxed{}$

7 Use the numbers 24, 55 and 31 to make two additions and two subtractions.

$\boxed{} + \boxed{} = \boxed{}$ $\boxed{} + \boxed{} = \boxed{}$

$\boxed{} - \boxed{} = \boxed{}$ $\boxed{} - \boxed{} = \boxed{}$

Key objective: Understand that subtraction is the inverse of addition; state the subtraction corresponding to a given addition and vice versa.

Name: **Date:**

Write in the missing numbers.

1 a $\boxed{80}$ — (-9) → $\boxed{}$ — $(+9)$ → $\boxed{}$

b $\boxed{}$ — (-15) → $\boxed{51}$ — $(+15)$ → $\boxed{}$

c $\boxed{}$ — (-40) → $\boxed{}$ — $(+40)$ → $\boxed{97}$

2 a $\boxed{50}$ — $(+28)$ → $\boxed{}$ — (-28) → $\boxed{}$

b $\boxed{}$ — $(+20)$ → $\boxed{87}$ — (-20) → $\boxed{}$

c $\boxed{}$ — $(+300)$ → $\boxed{}$ — (-300) → $\boxed{500}$

3 a $\boxed{} + 10 - 10 = 79$ **b** $60 + \boxed{} - 30 = 60$

4 a $\boxed{} - 9 + 9 = 16$ **b** $105 - 97 + \boxed{} = 105$

5 Find different pairs of numbers to make these statements true.

a $83 - \boxed{} + \boxed{} = 83$

b $83 - \boxed{} + \boxed{} = 83$

c $83 - \boxed{} + \boxed{} = 83$

Key objective: Know by heart all addition and subtraction facts for each number to at least 10.

Name: **Date:**

1   Write in the missing numbers.

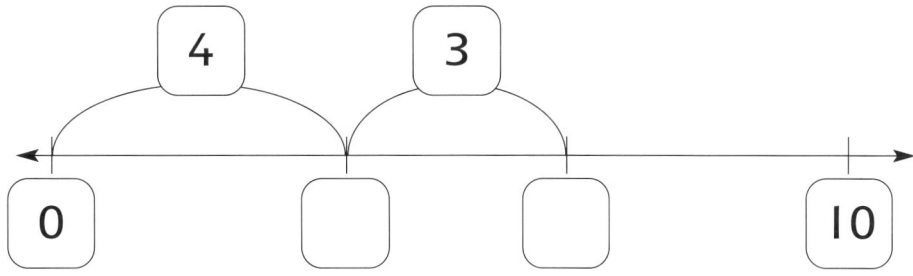

---

2   Write in the missing numbers in the grids.

addition

+	1	2	3	4	5
1	2				
2			5		
3					8
4					
5				9	

subtraction

−	1	2	3	4	5
6		4			
7				3	
8					
9			6		
10					5

---

3 **a** $3 + 2 =$ ☐   **b** $1 + 4 =$ ☐   **c** $3 + 1 =$ ☐

    d $2 + 4 =$ ☐   **e** $5 + 2 =$ ☐   **f** $3 + 3 =$ ☐

---

4 **a** $3 - 1 =$ ☐   **b** $4 - 2 =$ ☐   **c** $3 - 3 =$ ☐

    d $5 - 2 =$ ☐   **e** $2 - 1 =$ ☐   **f** $4 - 3 =$ ☐

Key objective: Know by heart all addition and subtraction facts for each number to at least 10.

Name: _____ **Date:** _____

1 Complete the addition grids.

a

+	2	6	4
3			
1			
4			

b

+	1	4	3
6			
2			
5			

2 Complete the subtraction grids.

a

–	3	0	1
6			
9			
4			

b

–	2	5	4
7			
5			
8			

3
a $8 + 1 =$ ☐
b $2 + 5 =$ ☐
c $5 + 0 =$ ☐

d $7 + 3 =$ ☐
e $3 + 3 =$ ☐
f $1 + 7 =$ ☐

g $0 + 9 =$ ☐
h $4 + 1 =$ ☐
i $9 + 1 =$ ☐

4
a $3 - 0 =$ ☐
b $10 - 4 =$ ☐
c $4 - 4 =$ ☐

d $8 - 6 =$ ☐
e $9 - 7 =$ ☐
f $7 - 3 =$ ☐

g $10 - 8 =$ ☐
h $6 - 5 =$ ☐
i $8 - 1 =$ ☐

5 Write in the sum of the two numbers.

number	2	0	5	3	2	8	4	5	7	0
number	8	7	2	0	6	1	3	5	2	10
sum	10									

6 Write in the difference between the two numbers.

number	2	10	5	9	4	10	3	8	9	7
number	0	3	1	4	2	6	2	3	9	6
difference	2									

7 Write in what the missing numbers could be.

a ⬜ + ⬜ = 5   **b** ⬜ + ⬜ = 8

c ⬜ + ⬜ = 10   **d** ⬜ + ⬜ = 6

8 Write in what the missing numbers could be.

a ⬜ − ⬜ = 4   **b** ⬜ − ⬜ = 7

c ⬜ − ⬜ = 6   **d** ⬜ − ⬜ = 9

9 **a** 2 plus 7 is ⬜   **b** 3 from 10 is ⬜

c 9 take away 6 is ⬜

d the sum of 8 and 2 is ⬜

Key objective: Know by heart all addition and subtraction facts for each number to at least 10.

Name: **Date:**

1 Write in the missing numbers in the grids.

a

+	5		
	8	4	
		1	6
	9		10

b

−			3
		9	6
	0	5	
	5		7

2 Write in the missing numbers in the grids.

a

number	2			3
number		2	0	
sum	9	8	9	10

b

number	6			8
number		7	9	
difference	4	0	1	1

3 Write in the missing numbers.

a $\boxed{} - 3 = 0$

b $9 - \boxed{} = 7$

c $2 + \boxed{} = 4$

d $\boxed{} + 6 = 10$

4 Write in different pairs of numbers.

$\boxed{} + \boxed{} = 10$ $\boxed{} - \boxed{} = 4$

$\boxed{} + \boxed{} = 10$ $\boxed{} - \boxed{} = 4$

$\boxed{} + \boxed{} = 10$ $\boxed{} - \boxed{} = 4$

Key objective: Use knowledge that addition can be done in any order to do mental calculations more efficiently.

Name: **Date:**

1   **a** $17 + 4 =$ ☐   **b** $4 + 17 =$ ☐

    c $3 + 19 =$ ☐   **d** $19 + 3 =$ ☐

2   **a** $20 + 40 =$ ☐   **b** $40 + 20 =$ ☐

    c $30 + 10 =$ ☐   **d** $10 + 30 =$ ☐

3   **a** $1 + 9 + 5 =$ ☐   **b** $9 + 5 + 1 =$ ☐

    c $3 + 9 + 2 =$ ☐   **d** $9 + 3 + 2 =$ ☐

4   Find the sum of 13 and 12. ☐

Write about how you did it.

....

....

5   Find the sum of $3 + 6 + 7$. ☐

Write about how you did it.

....

....

Key objective: Use knowledge that addition can be done in any order to do mental calculations more efficiently.

Name: **Date:**

Find the answers to the additions and write about how you did them.

1   5 + 28 = ☐

....

....

....

2   30 + 90 = ☐

....

....

....

3   7 + 50 = ☐

....

....

....

4   6 + 400 = ☐

....

....

....

5 17 + 30 = ☐

6 38 + 14 = ☐

7 49 + 10 = ☐

8 200 + 700 = ☐

9 7 + 9 + 3 = ☐

Written assessment 5C

Name: | **Date:**

1 a $4 + \boxed{} = 43$ **b** $\boxed{} + 38 = 45$

2 a $7 + \boxed{} = 57$ **b** $\boxed{} + 40 = 48$

3 a $5 + \boxed{} = 505$ **b** $\boxed{} + 600 = 609$

4 a $16 + \boxed{} = 76$ **b** $12 + \boxed{} = 92$

5 a $14 + \boxed{} = 55$ **b** $11 + \boxed{} = 84$

6 a $10 + \boxed{} = 72$ **b** $\boxed{} + 33 = 43$

7 a $20 + \boxed{} = 80$ **b** $30 + \boxed{} = 90$

8 a $40 + \boxed{} = 100$ **b** $20 + \boxed{} = 100$

9 a $30 + \boxed{} = 92$ **b** $\boxed{} + 57 = 77$

10 a $8 + \boxed{} + 2 = 15$ **b** $\boxed{} + 7 + 3 = 19$

Key objective: Understand the operation of multiplication as repeated addition or as describing an array.

Name: **Date:**

1

  a   How many pennies in each purse? ☐

  b   How many pennies altogether? ☐

  c   How many pence is 3 lots of 2p? ☐ p

  d   How many pence is 3 × 2p? ☐ p

2

  a   How many buns in each row? ☐

  b   How many buns in each column? ☐

  c   How many buns altogether? ☐

  d   How many is 3 lots of 4? ☐

  e   How many is 4 lots of 3? ☐

  f   What is 3 × 4? ☐   **g**   What is 4 × 3? ☐

3 a   5 + 5 + 5 = ☐   **b**   3 lots of 5 = ☐

  c   3 × 5 = ☐

Key objective: Understand the operation of multiplication as repeated addition or as describing an array.

Name: **Date:**

I a How many fish in each bowl?

b How many bowls?

c How many fish altogether?

d How many is 2 lots of 4 fish?

e What is 2 × 4?

2 a How many windows in each row?

b How many windows in each column?

c How many windows altogether?

d How many is 3 lots of 5?

e How many is 5 lots of 3?

f What is 3 × 5?

g What is 5 × 3?

3 Write in the missing numbers.

    a 4 + 4 + 4 = ◻   **b** 3 lots of 4 = ◻

    c 3 + 3 + 3 + 3 = ◻   **d** 4 lots of 3 = ◻

---

4 Write in the missing numbers.

    a 5 + 5 + 5 + 5 = 4 lots of ◻ = ◻

    b 6 + 6 + 6 = ◻ lots of 6 = ◻

    c 2 + 2 + 2 + 2 + 2 = ◻ lots of ◻ = ◻

---

5 **a** On the grid, colour in a rectangle that is six squares long and three squares wide.

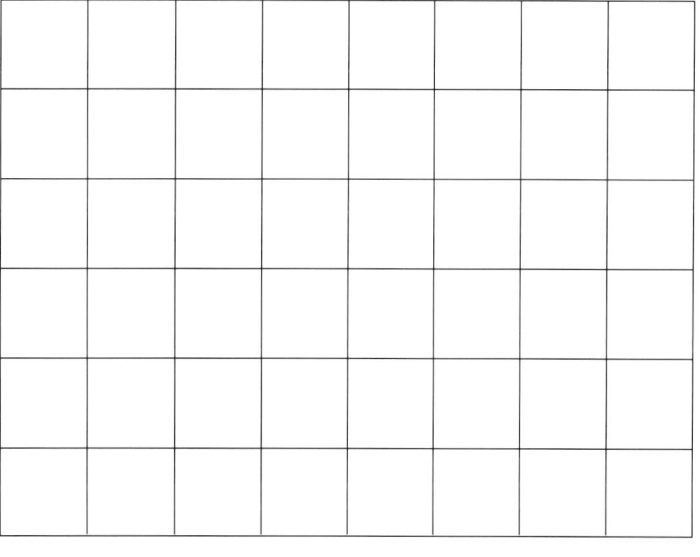

    b How many is 3 × 6? ◻

---

6 Write in the missing numbers.

    a 7 + 7 + 7 = ◻ × 7 = ◻

    b 6 + 6 + 6 + 6 = 4 × ◻ = ◻

    c 8 + 8 + 8 + 8 + 8 = ◻ × ◻ = ◻

Key objective: Understand the operation of multiplication as repeated addition or as describing an array.

Name: ⬚ **Date:** ⬚

1 **a** 3 lots of 2 = ⬚ + ⬚ + ⬚ = ⬚

b 6 lots of ⬚ = 3 + 3 + 3 + 3 + 3 + 3 = ⬚

c ⬚ lots of 5 = 5 + 5 + 5 = ⬚

d ⬚ lots of ⬚ = 4 + 4 + 4 + 4 + 4 = ⬚

2 **a** 4 lots of 6 = ⬚ × 6 = ⬚

b 8 lots of 5 = 8 × ⬚ = ⬚

c 10 lots of 3 = ⬚ × ⬚ = ⬚

3 **a** 4 × 7 = ⬚ lots of 7 = ⬚

b 5 × 4 = 5 lots of ⬚ = ⬚

c 2 lots of 8 = ⬚ × ⬚ = ⬚

4 **a** 5 lots of 6 = 6 lots of ⬚ = ⬚

b 3 lots of ⬚ = 7 lots of 3 = ⬚

c ⬚ lots of 9 = ⬚ lots of 2 = ⬚

Key objective: Know and use halving as the inverse of doubling.

Name: **Date:**

Write in the missing numbers.

1 **a** 10 → halve → ◻   **b** 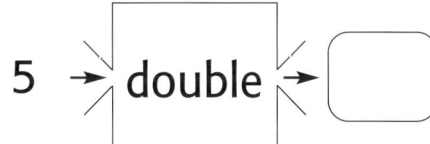 5 → double → ◻

2 **a** 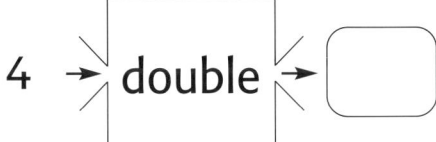 4 → double → ◻   **b**  8 → halve → ◻

3
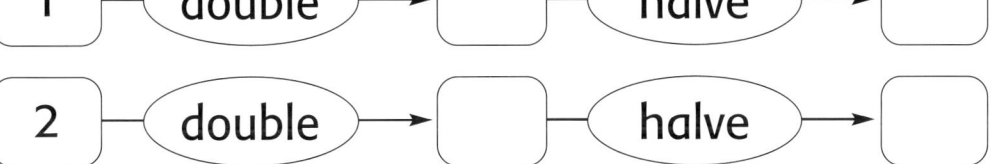
1 — double → ◻ — halve → ◻

2 — double → ◻ — halve → ◻

3 — double → ◻ — halve → ◻

4 — double → ◻ — halve → ◻

4
10 — halve → ◻ — double → ◻

8 — halve → ◻ — double → ◻

6 — halve → ◻ — double → ◻

4 — halve → ◻ — double → ◻

Key objective: Know and use halving as the inverse of doubling.

Name: | **Date:**

Write in the missing numbers.

1 a

12 → double → ☐ → halve → ☐

b

20 → halve → ☐ → double → ☐

2

halve	3							
number	**6**	**14**	**4**	**10**	**30**	**18**	**20**	**50**
double	12							

3

13 → multiply by 2 → ☐ → divide by 2 → ☐

25 → multiply by 2 → ☐ → divide by 2 → ☐

9 → multiply by 2 → ☐ → divide by 2 → ☐

45 → multiply by 2 → ☐ → divide by 2 → ☐

35 → multiply by 2 → ☐ → divide by 2 → ☐

Write in the missing numbers.

4

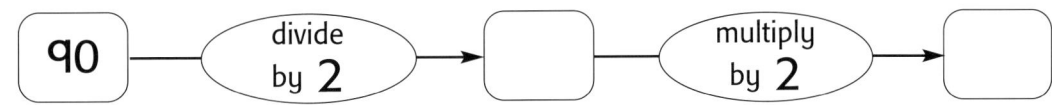

---

5 **a** Double 17 is 34. So a half of 34 is ☐

   b Double 60 is 120. So a half of 120 is ☐

   c Double 22 is 44. So a half of 44 is ☐

   d Double 100 is 200. So a half of 200 is ☐

---

6 **a** A half of 38 is 19. So double 19 is ☐

   b A half of 70 is 35. So double 35 is ☐

   c A half of 46 is 23. So double 23 is ☐

   d A half of 300 is 150. So double 150 is ☐

Key objective: Know and use halving as the inverse of doubling.

Name: **Date:**

Write what the missing numbers could be.

1

☐ — double → 16 — halve → ☐

☐ — double → ☐ — halve → 35

2

☐ — halve → 7 — double → ☐

☐ — halve → ☐ — double → 50

3

halve	6		2		15			150
number	**12**	**40**						
double	24			28		36	90	

4

☐ — ×2 → ☐ — ÷2 → 8

☐ — ×2 → ☐ — ÷2 → ☐

5

☐ — ÷2 → 16 — ×2 → ☐

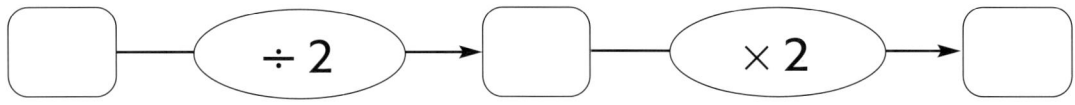

☐ — ÷2 → ☐ — ×2 → ☐

Key objective: Know by heart facts for the 2 and 10 multiplication tables.

Name: **Date:**

1   Haroon has four 2p coins.

How much money has Haroon? ☐ p

2   The letter balances five 10 g weights.

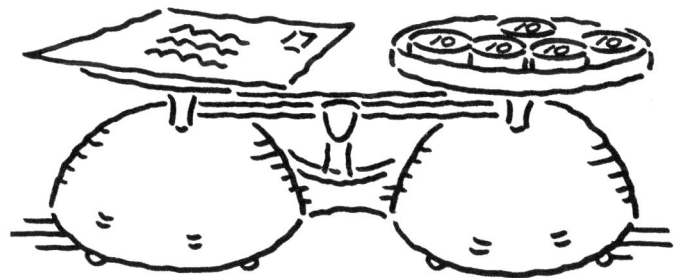

How many grams does the letter weigh? ☐ g

3   Jill has seven 10p coins.

How much money has Jill? ☐ p

4 **a** $1 \times 2 =$ ☐   **b** $4 \times 2 =$ ☐

    c $2 \times 2 =$ ☐   **d** $3 \times 2 =$ ☐

5 **a** $1 \times 10 =$ ☐   **b** $3 \times 10 =$ ☐

    c $4 \times 10 =$ ☐   **d** $2 \times 10 =$ ☐

Key objective: Know by heart facts for the 2 and 10 multiplication tables.

Name: **Date:**

1 Write in the missing numbers in the grids.

a

×	2	10
4	8	
7		
3		
1		
5		

b

×	2	10
10		
2		
9		
8		
6		

2 a $5 \times 2 =$ ☐ **b** $1 \times 2 =$ ☐ **c** $8 \times 2 =$ ☐

d $3 \times 2 =$ ☐ **e** $9 \times 2 =$ ☐ **f** $4 \times 2 =$ ☐

g $7 \times 2 =$ ☐ **h** $2 \times 2 =$ ☐ **i** $6 \times 2 =$ ☐

3 a $5 \times 10 =$ ☐ **b** $9 \times 10 =$ ☐

c $6 \times 10 =$ ☐ **d** $2 \times 10 =$ ☐

e $8 \times 10 =$ ☐ **f** $3 \times 10 =$ ☐

4 a Three twos = ☐ **b** 4 times 10 = ☐

c 6 times 2 = ☐ **d** Seven tens = ☐

5 In each pile, every coin is a 2p.

pile A   pile B

How much more money is in pile A than in pile B? ☐ p

6 All the coins in the purses are 10p.

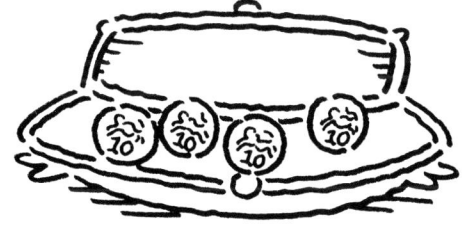

purse A   purse B

How much more money
is in purse A than in purse B? ☐ p

7 a $2 \times 5 =$ ☐   **b** $2 \times 6 =$ ☐

c $2 \times 8 =$ ☐   **d** $2 \times 3 =$ ☐

e $2 \times 9 =$ ☐   **f** $2 \times 4 =$ ☐

g $2 \times 7 =$ ☐   **h** $2 \times 10 =$ ☐

8 a $10 \times 7 =$ ☐   **b** $10 \times 9 =$ ☐

c $10 \times 6 =$ ☐   **d** $10 \times 4 =$ ☐

e $10 \times 8 =$ ☐   **f** $10 \times 3 =$ ☐

Key objective: Know by heart facts for the 2 and 10 multiplication tables.

Name: Date:

Write in the missing numbers.

1

×	3			
2	6			2
10		90	40	

×				
10	80	20		
2			10	12

2 **a** $4 \times \boxed{} = 8$ **b** $\boxed{} \times 9 = 18$

     c $\boxed{} \times 2 = 12$ **d** $\boxed{} \times 2 = 14$

     e $2 \times \boxed{} = 20$ **f** $8 \times \boxed{} = 16$

3 **a** $\boxed{} \times 10 = 70$ **b** $3 \times \boxed{} = 30$

     c $\boxed{} \times 8 = 80$ **d** $10 \times \boxed{} = 60$

     e $\boxed{} \times 10 = 90$ **f** $\boxed{} \times 10 = 50$

4 Write in the missing numbers or number names.

     a Five .... are ten.

     b $\boxed{}$ times 2 is 14.

     c .... tens are 100.

     d 2 multiplied by $\boxed{}$ is 6.

Key objective: Estimate, measure and compare lengths, masses and capacities, using standard units; suggest suitable units and equipment for such measurements.

Name: **Date:**

1

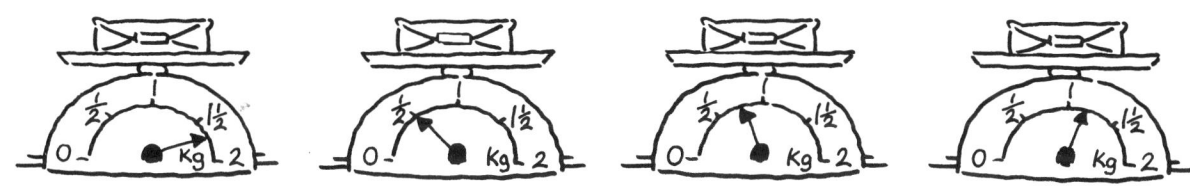

1 metre

a   Tick (✓) each stick that is longer than 1 metre.

b   Cross (✗) each stick that is shorter than 1 metre.

2

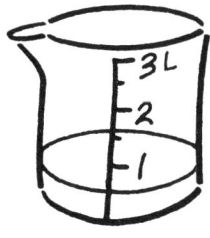 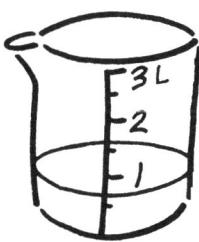 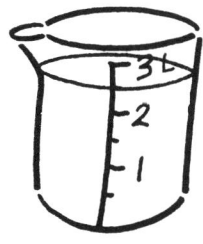 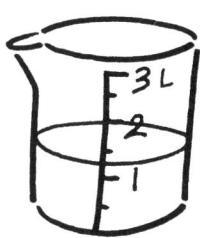

a   Tick (✓) each parcel that is heavier than 1 kilogram.

b   Cross (✗) each parcel that is lighter than 1 kilogram.

3

a   Tick (✓) each jug that contains more than 1 litre.

b   Cross (✗) each jug that contains less than 1 litre.

Key objective: Estimate, measure and compare lengths, masses and capacities, using standard units; suggest suitable units and equipment for such measurements.

Name: _____ **Date:** _____

1 a Write in the height of each child.

b Tick (✓) the child who is the tallest.

c Cross (✗) the child who is the shortest.

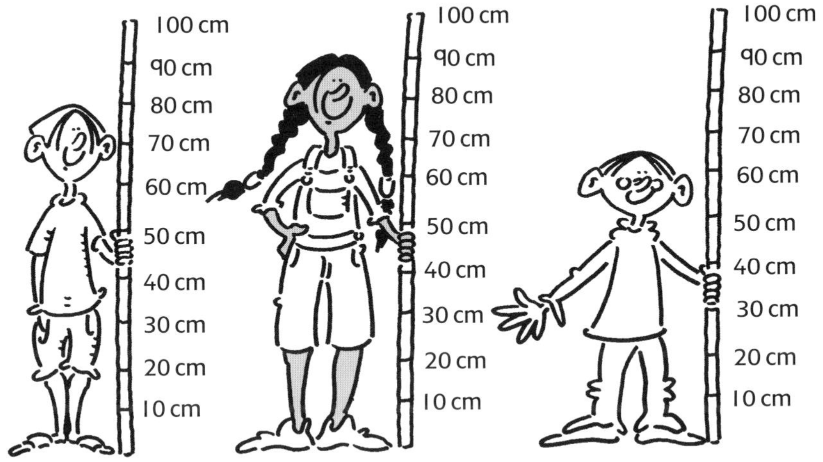

Sebastian [ ] cm
Mara [ ] cm
Bruce [ ] cm

2

[ ] cubes   [ ] cubes   [ ] cubes

a Write in how heavy each trainer is in cubes.

b Tick (✓) the trainer that is the heaviest.

c Cross (✗) the trainer that is the lightest.

3 It takes four glasses to fill the 1 litre bottle.

How many glasses are needed to fill a 2 litre bottle? [ ]

4 This is a matchstick.

Estimate how many of these matchsticks will fit along the longer side of this page. ⬜

5 Tick (✓) an object it would be sensible to measure in centimetres.

ladybird   cat   mountain   river

6 Tick (✓) the object it would be sensible to weigh in kilograms.

cup   robin   lorry   fly

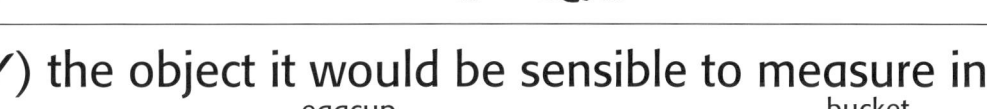

7 Tick (✓) the object it would be sensible to measure in litres.

thimble   eggcup   spoon   bucket

8 Circle the unit you would use to measure:

a the height of a building.

| kilograms | litres | metres |

b the amount of petrol in a car's tank.

| kilograms | litres | metres |

c the weight of a log from a tree.

| kilograms | litres | metres |

Key objective: Estimate, measure and compare lengths, masses and capacities, using standard units; suggest suitable units and equipment for such measurements.

Name: **Date:**

1 A tree trunk is 10 metres long.

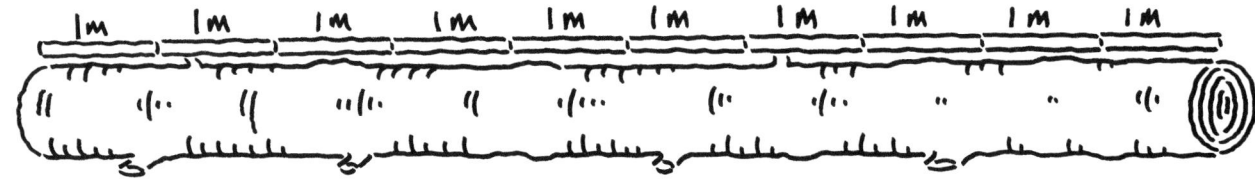

   a What is the length of two trunks? ☐ m

   b One trunk is cut into halves.

     How many metres long is one-half of the trunk? ☐ m

2 A bag of potatoes weighs 6 kilograms.

   a What is the weight of two bags of potatoes? ☐ kg

   b What is the weight of half a bag of potatoes? ☐ kg

3 A kettle holds 4 litres of water.

   a How many litres will two kettles hold? ☐ L

   b How many litres will the kettle hold when it is half full? ☐ L

Key objective: Read a simple scale to the nearest labelled division, including using a ruler to draw and measure lines to the nearest centimetre.

Name: _____ **Date:** _____

1

☐ cm   ☐ cm   ☐ cm

What is the height of each toy?

2

☐ kg   ☐ kg   ☐ kg

What is the weight on each scale?

3

☐ L   ☐ L   ☐ L

How many litres in each jug?

Key objective: Read a simple scale to the nearest labelled division, including using a ruler to draw and measure lines to the nearest centimetre.

Name: **Date:**

1   Measure the lengths of the lines.

a   _____   ☐ cm

b   _____

☐ cm

c

☐ cm

---

2   Measure the distance between each pair of flags.

a   ☐ cm

b   ☐ cm

3

stick a

0 1 2 3 4 5 6 7 8 9 10
cm

stick b

About how long is each stick?

Stick **a** is about ☐ cm.   Stick **b** is about ☐ cm.

4 Write in the missing numbers in the sentences.

a The apples weigh just more than ☐ kg.

b The oranges weigh nearly ☐ kg.

c The carrots weigh ☐ and a bit kilograms.

5 Write in the missing numbers in the sentences.

a The jug contains just less than ☐ litres.

b The kettle contains about ☐ litres.

c The bucket contains ☐ and a bit litres.

6 Write in the weight of each parcel.

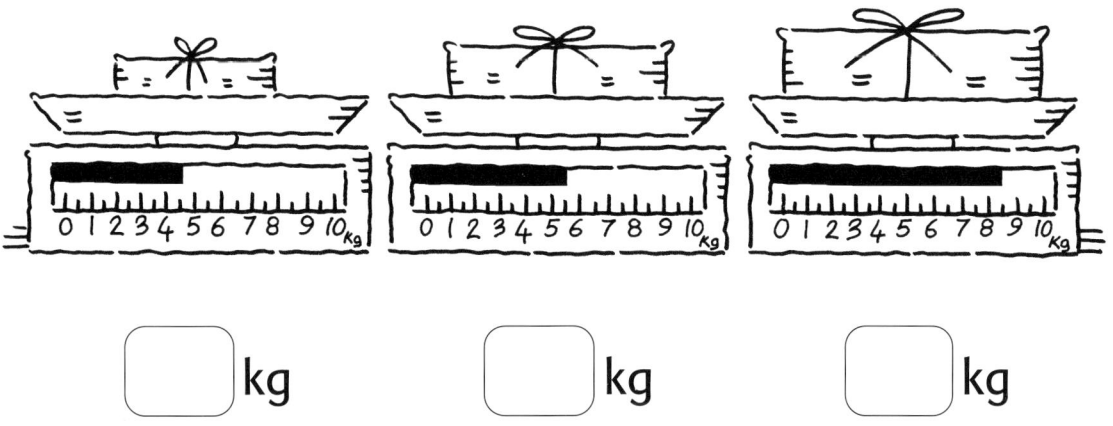

☐ kg   ☐ kg   ☐ kg

Key objective: Read a simple scale to the nearest labelled division, including using a ruler to draw and measure lines to the nearest centimetre.

Name: **Date:**

1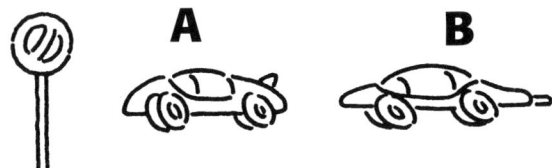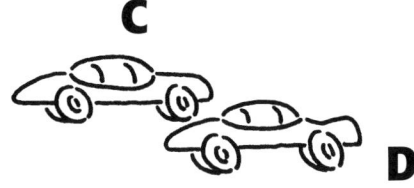

A   B   C

D

   a How far is car **A** from the winning post? ☐ cm

   b How far is car **D** from the winning post? ☐ cm

   c What is the distance between cars **B** and **C**? ☐ cm

2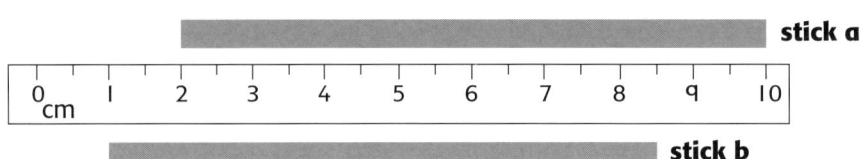

stick a

0 1 2 3 4 5 6 7 8 9 10
cm

stick b

What is the length of each stick?

Stick **a** is ☐ cm.   Stick **b** is ☐ cm.

3 Luke weighs out 3 kg of sugar.

He uses $1\frac{1}{2}$ kg of it.

Draw the pointer on the scale to show the weight of the sugar that is left.

4 Sita makes 4 litres of lemonade. She drinks 1 litre of it.

Draw a line on the jug to show how much is left.

Key objective: Use the mathematical names for common 2D and 3D shapes; sort shapes and describe some of their features.

Name: _____ Date: _____

I   Match each shape to its name.

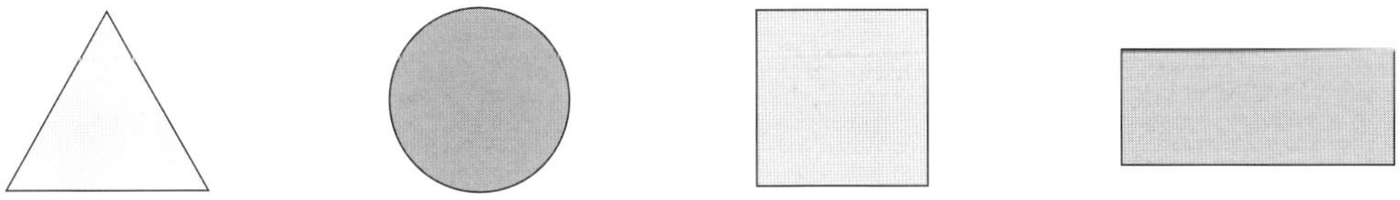

circle   square   rectangle   triangle

2   Match each solid to its name.

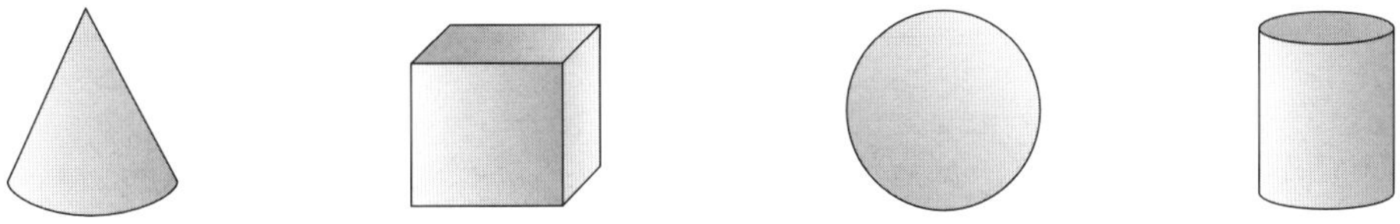

cube   cylinder   cone   sphere

3   Match each shape to its number of corners.

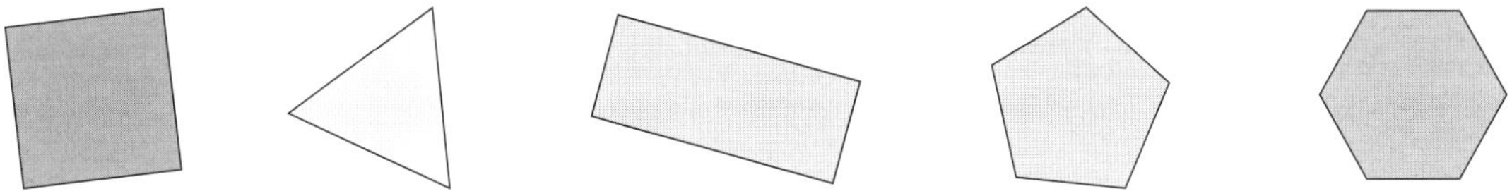

3 corners   4 corners   5 corners   6 corners

4   Tick (✓) each shape that is sorted wrongly.

| triangles | 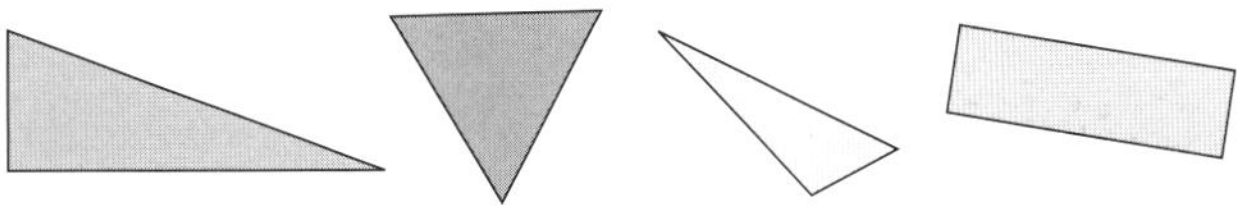 |
| rectangles | 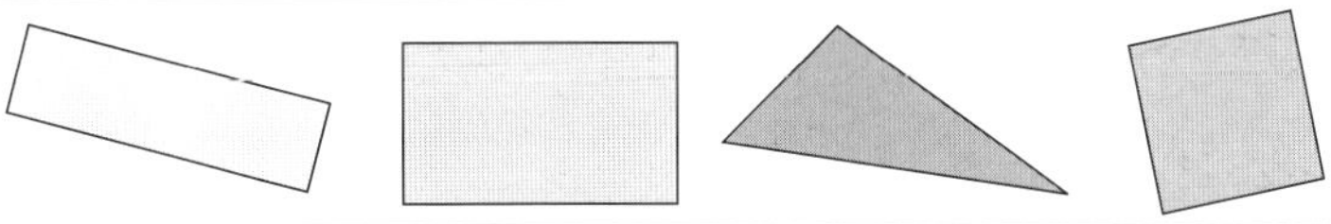 |

Key objective: Use the mathematical names for common 2D and 3D shapes; sort shapes and describe some of their features.

Name: **Date:**

I Match each shape to its name.

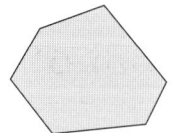 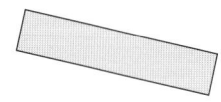 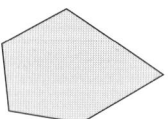 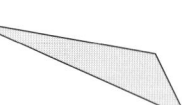 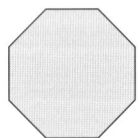

rectangle   triangle   hexagon   octagon   pentagon

2 Match each solid to its name.

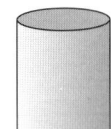 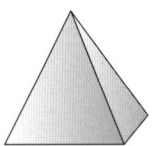 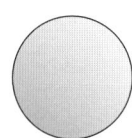 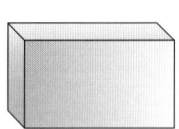 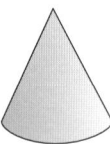

sphere   cone   cuboid   pyramid   cylinder

3 Complete each shape.

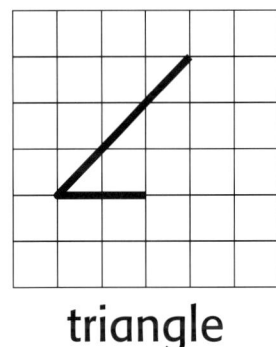

triangle

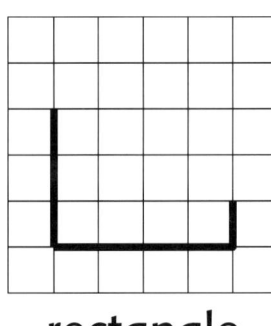

rectangle

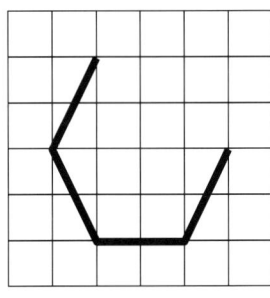

hexagon

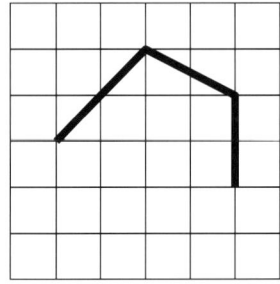

pentagon

4 Match each shape to a property.

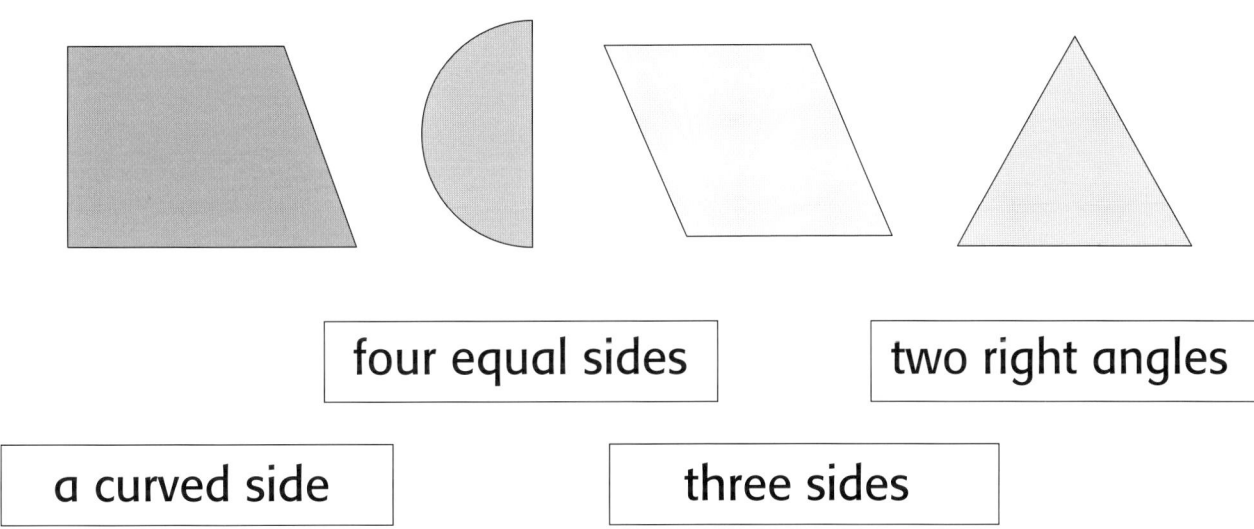

| four equal sides | | two right angles |

| a curved side | | three sides |

5 Write in the missing numbers in the grid.

	number of flat faces	number of curved faces	number of edges
cone		1	
cuboid			12
pyramid		0	8
cylinder	2		

6 Tick (✓) the two shapes which have sides that are all the same length.

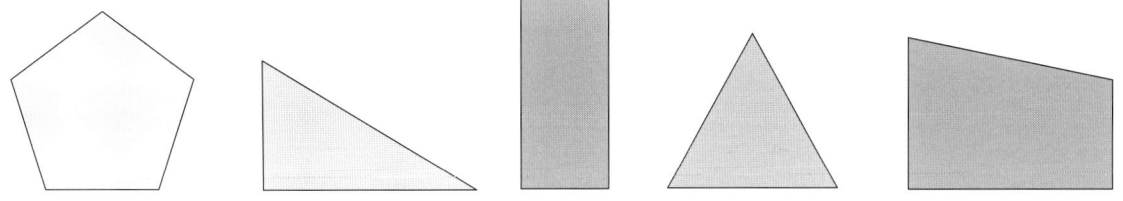

Key objective: Use the mathematical names for common 2D and 3D shapes; sort shapes and describe some of their features.

Name: **Date:**

1 Complete each shape.

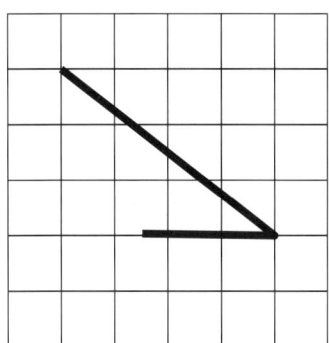 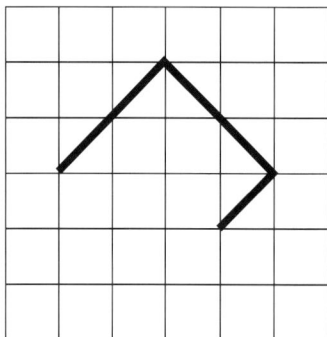 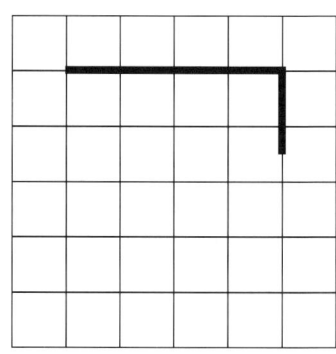

| a right-angled triangle | has four equal sides | has four sides and one right angle |

2 Write in the missing numbers.

	number of flat faces	number of corners	number of edges
a triangular prism			
a hemisphere			
a square pyramid			

3 Write the letters in the sorting diagram to show where each shape belongs.

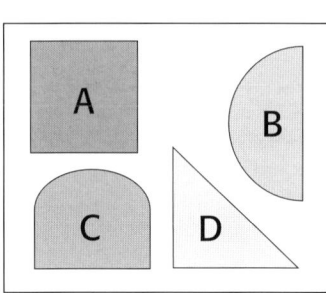 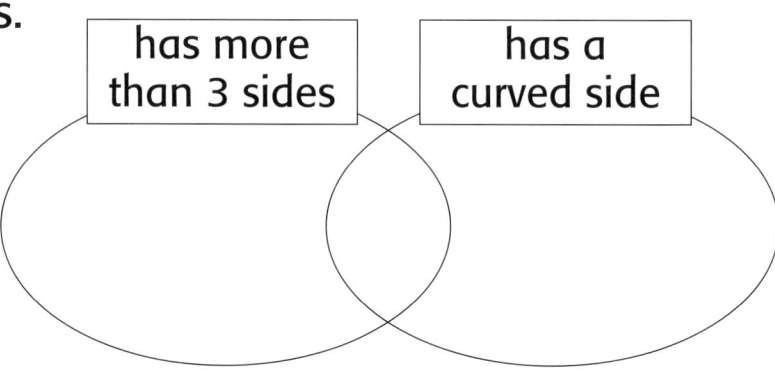

has more than 3 sides

has a curved side

Key objective: Use mathematical vocabulary to describe position, direction and movement.

Name: **Date:**

1 **a** Draw a triangle in the square immediately above the car.

     b Draw a circle in a square in front of the car.

     c Draw a cross in a square on the edge of the grid.

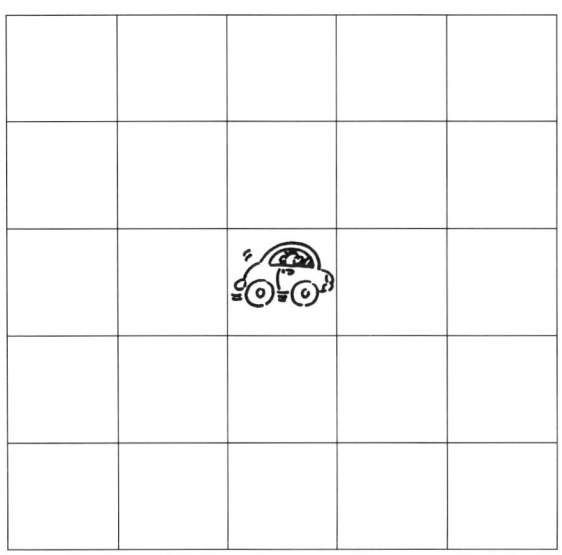

2 The crayon is moved two squares to the right.

    Draw the crayon in its new position.

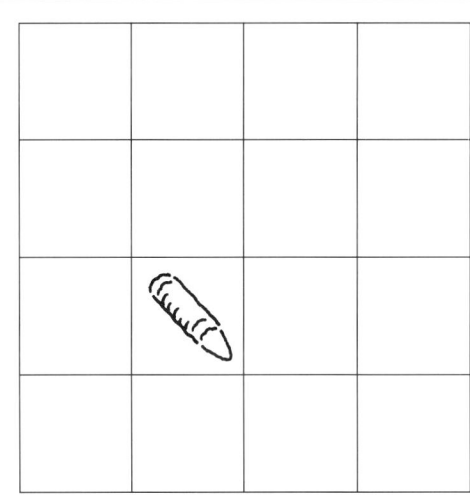

3 The arrow is turned to face the opposite direction.

    Draw the new position of the arrow.

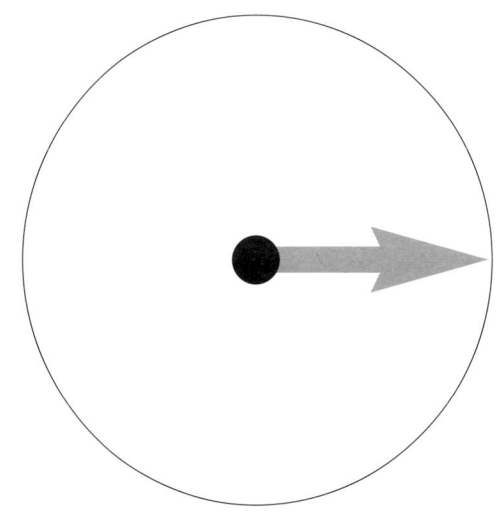

Key objective: Use mathematical vocabulary to describe position, direction and movement.

Name: **Date:**

1   Ride the bicycle along the path to the house.

Complete the list of moves that it makes.

right 3

up 3

....

....

....

2   Use these words to complete the sentences.

right   **edge**   **below**

     next   **above**

a   The girl is .... to the fire engine.

b   The fire engine is .... the ambulance.

c   The boat is on the .... of the grid.

d   The house is on the .... of the fire engine.

3 Follow the instructions to turn each arrow. Draw each arrow's new position.

a $\frac{1}{4}$ turn clockwise

b $\frac{1}{2}$ turn anticlockwise

c 3 right angles anticlockwise

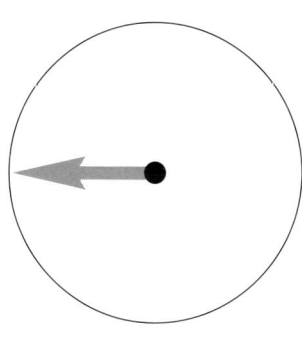 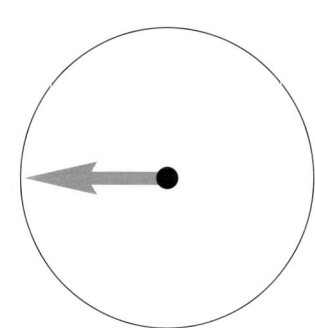 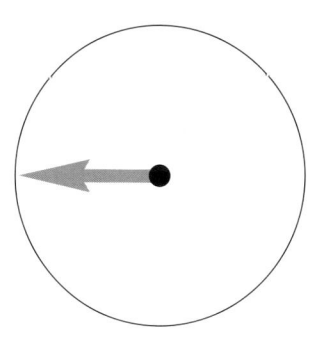

4 **a** Move the circle 2 squares right and 1 square down.

Draw it in its new position.

b Move the triangle 3 squares left and 2 squares up.

Draw it in its new position.

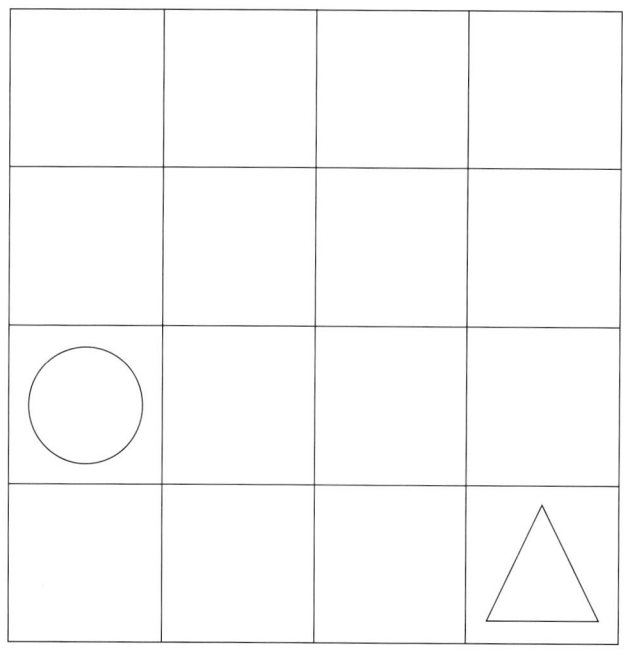

5 Each triangle is turned clockwise through a right angle. Draw each new triangle.

a

b

c

 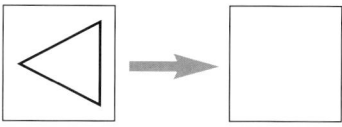

Key objective: Use mathematical vocabulary to describe position, direction and movement.

Name: **Date:**

1 The dog wants to reach the boy. It moves **2 squares to the right followed by 1 square up**. It keeps doing this until it reaches the boy. Draw the dog's path.

2 Use these words to complete the sentences.

down   **up**   **left**   **right**

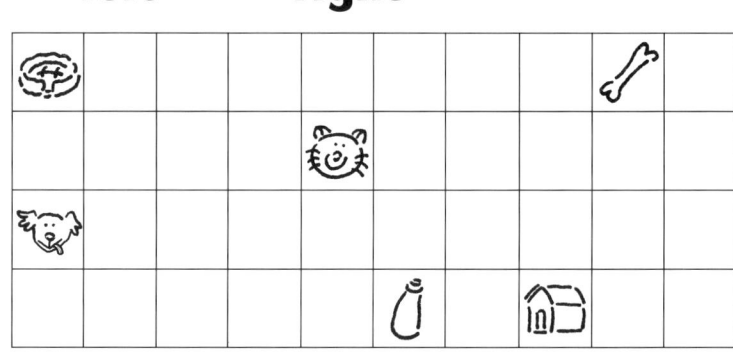

a The dog is 7 squares .... and 1 square .... from the kennel.

b To get the milk the cat moves 1 square .... and 2 squares ....

c To get the bone the dog moves 2 squares .... and 8 squares ....

3 The triangle is moved **2 squares to the right** and is then **turned clockwise through 1 right angle**. This is repeated **three** times.

Draw the triangle each time it is moved.

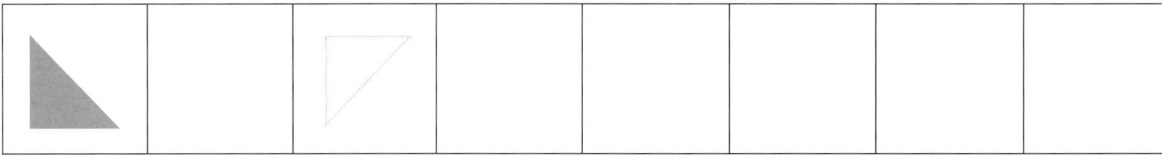

Key objective: Choose and use appropriate operations and efficient calculation strategies to solve problems, explaining how the problem was solved.

Name: **Date:**

1   Write the signs + or – in the circles to make each calculation correct.

    a $2 \bigcirc 1 = 1$

    b $3 \bigcirc 2 = 5$

    c $4 \bigcirc 3 = 1$

---

2   Make up a number story for this addition.

    $1 + 1 = 2$

    ....

    ....

    ....

---

3   Find the answer to $4 + 5$. $\boxed{}$

    Write about how you did it.

    ....

    ....

    ....

Key objective: Choose and use appropriate operations and efficient calculation strategies to solve problems, explaining how the problem was solved.

Name: **Date:**

1 Write the signs +, – or × in the circles to make the calculations correct.

a $20 \bigcirc 2 = 18$

b $20 \bigcirc 2 = 22$

c $20 \bigcirc 2 = 40$

2 Make up a number story for this addition. $15 + 21 = 36$

....

....

....

....

3 Make up a number story for this subtraction. $37 - 6 = 31$

....

....

....

....

4 Write the signs +, – or × in the circles to make each calculation correct.

a 30 ◯ 10 = 15 ◯ 5

b 2 ◯ 10 = 10 ◯ 10

5 Find the answer to 22 – 5. ▢

Write about how you did it.

....

....

....

6 Find the answer to 31 + 22. ▢

Write about how you did it.

....

....

....

7 Find the answer to 3 × 10. ▢

Write about how you did it.

....

....

....

Key objective: Choose and use appropriate operations and efficient calculation strategies to solve problems, explaining how the problem was solved.

Name: **Date:**

1 Write the signs +, ×, − or = in the circles to make the calculations correct.

a 3 ◯ 6 ◯ 10 ◯ 1

b 20 ◯ 2 ◯ 10 ◯ 30

c 14 ◯ 8 ◯ 2 ◯ 3

2 Make up a number story for this calculation.

$5 \times 2 - 3 = 7$

....

....

....

3 Find the answer to 42 − 18 + 26. ▢

Write about how you did it.

....

....

....

Name: **Date:**

Part A

Score   out of 28

1 a There are 2 pies in every box.

How many pies are there in 7 boxes? ☐

b There are 10 Bonzo cards in every pack.

How many cards are
there altogether in 4 packs? ☐

---

2 a Write in on the number track where 32 should be.

		25	26	27	28				

b Count on in tens from 20 to 80.

How many tens did you count? ☐

---

3 Shade the odd numbers in this grid.

3	6	9
12	15	18
21	24	27
30	33	36

4 Continue the sequence.

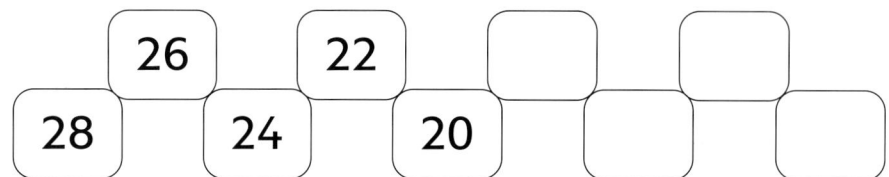

26 22

28 24 20

5 Write in the three missing numbers in this sequence.

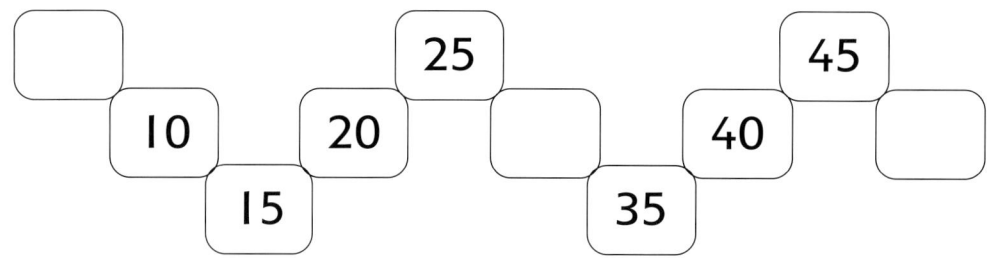

25 45

10 20 40

15 35

6 Write the missing numbers and number names.

18 ⬍

⬍

37 ⬍

⬍

.... seventy-three   .... eighty-one

7 Wasim has 43p in 10p and 1p coins.

Put ticks (✓) on coins to make 43p.

8 Write in numbers to make the additions correct.

a 82 = ☐ + 2   **b** 59 = 50 + ◯

c △ = 10 + ☐

9 Write the four numbers in the oval in order, largest first.

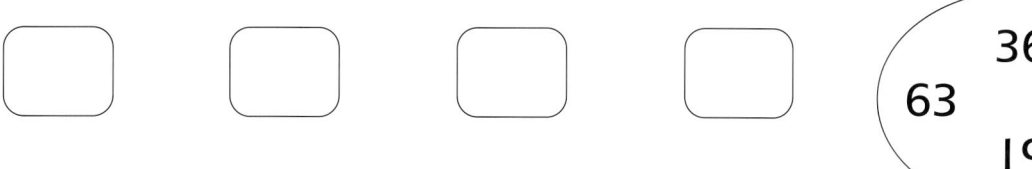

largest   smallest

10 Find the missing numbers.

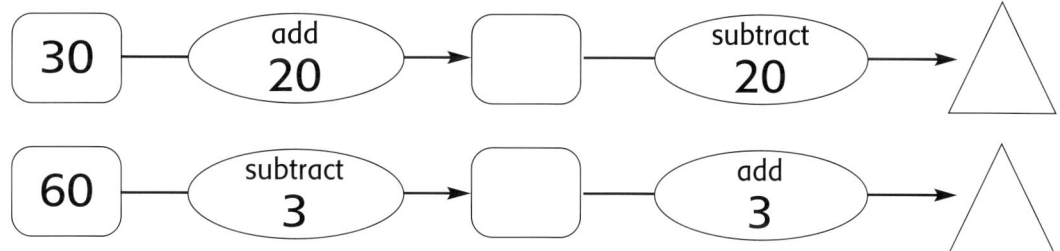

Explain why the number in the triangle is the same as the start number.

....

....

11 Complete the addition and subtraction grids.

a

+	3	8	5
2			
7			
5			

b

–	4	1	6
9			
7			
10			

12 Write in the missing numbers.

a $27 + 9 = 9 + \boxed{} = \boxed{}$

b $30 + \boxed{} = 50 + 30 = \boxed{}$

13 Write in the missing numbers.

10 + 10 + 10 = 3 lots of ☐ = ☐

2 + 2 + 2 + 2 = 4 × ☐ = ☐

14 Complete the sentence.

There are 3 lots of ☐ buns in the box.

15 Find the missing numbers.

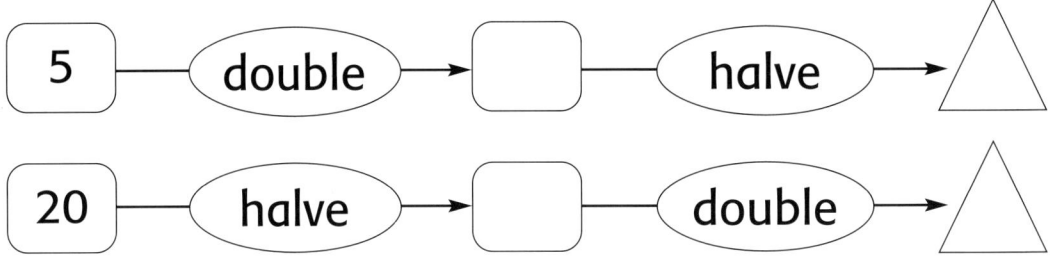

Explain why the number in the triangle is the same as the start number.

....

....

....

16 Complete the multiplication grids.

a

×	3	5	2	4
2				
10				

b

×	8	7	9	6
10				
2				

17 Write a number story for the multiplication $2 \times 7 = 14$.

....

....

18 Write the signs +, − or × in the circles to make the calculations correct.

10 ◯ 9 = 1   10 ◯ 9 = 90   10 ◯ 9 = 19

19 Match the object to the correct box.

| length of a pencil |
| height of a house |
| length of a worm |
| height of your teacher |
| length of your leg |

| shorter than 1 metre |

| longer than 1 metre |

20 Draw lines to show where the objects belong.

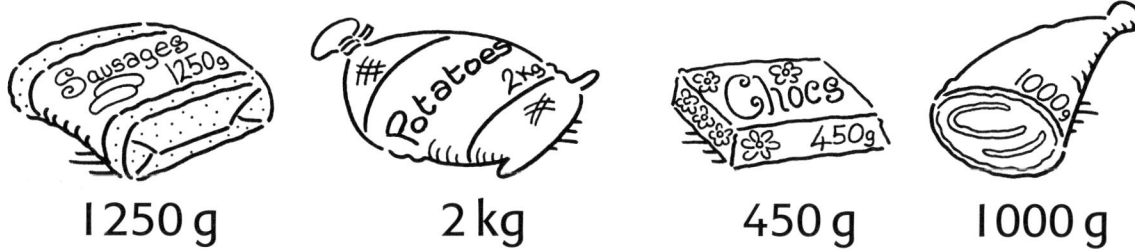

1250 g   2 kg   450 g   1000 g

| less than 1 kilogram | | equal to 1 kilogram | | more than 1 kilogram |

21 Match each container to the amount you think a real
one would hold.

200 L   200 mL   1 L   10 L   10 mL

22 What is the height of each object?

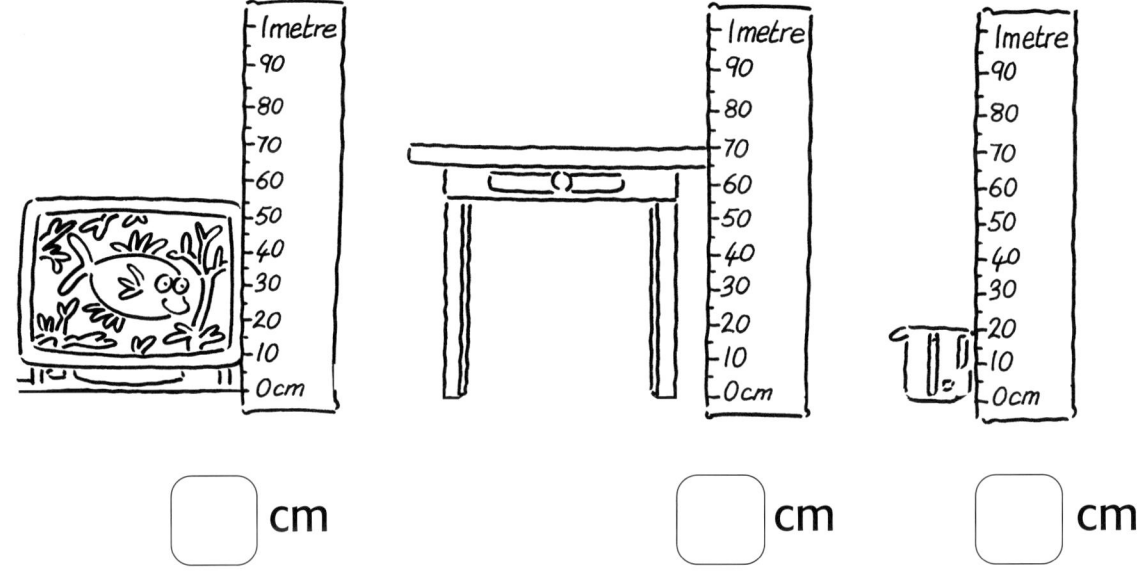

☐ cm   ☐ cm   ☐ cm

23 Write how heavy each parcel is.

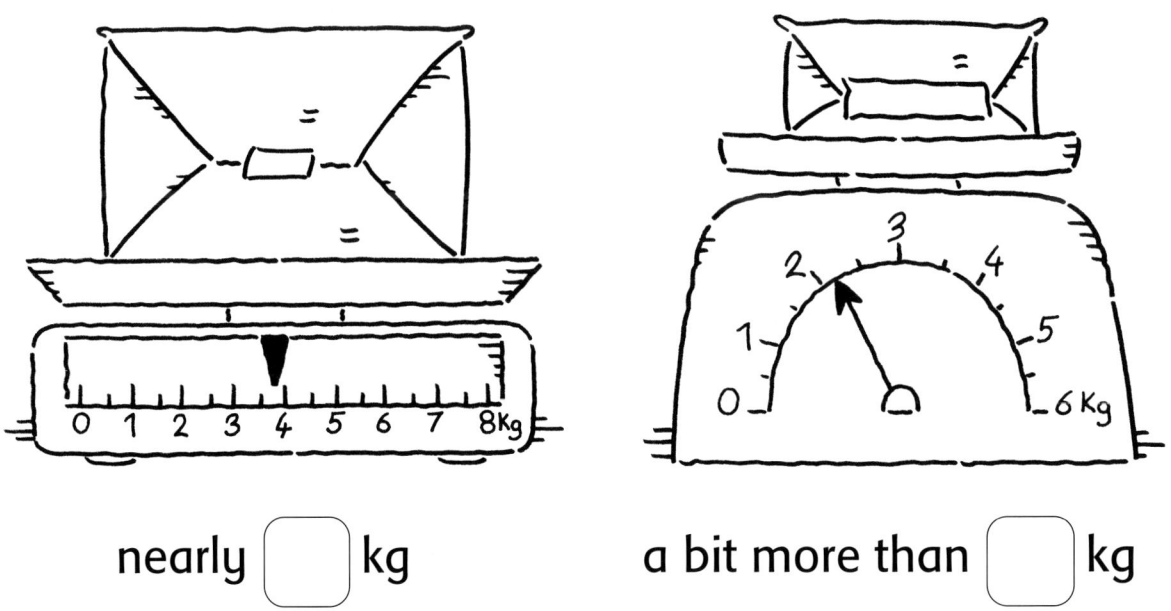

nearly ☐ kg   a bit more than ☐ kg

24 Measure the distance between the bottom of each pair of posts.

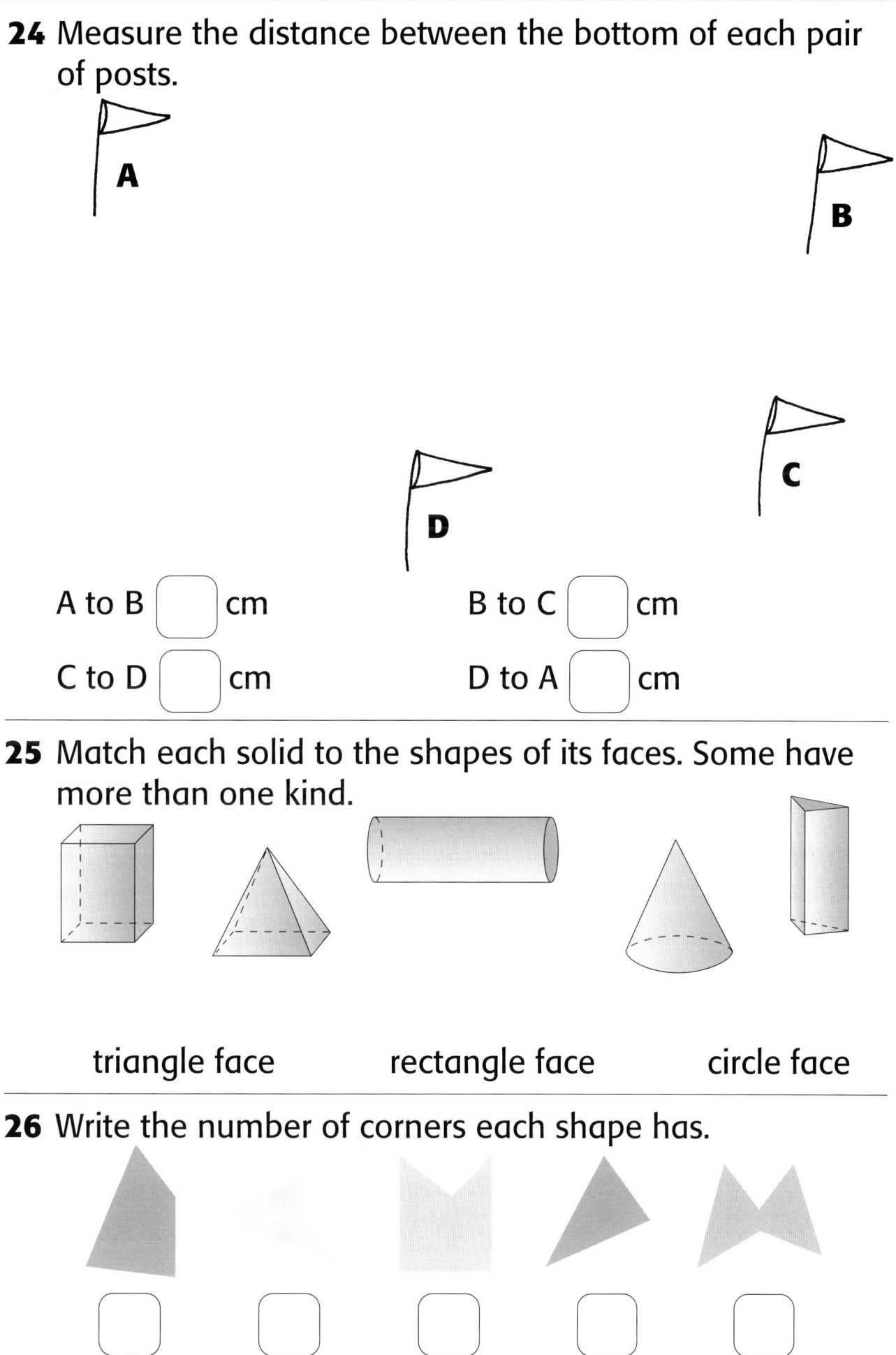

A to B ☐ cm   B to C ☐ cm

C to D ☐ cm   D to A ☐ cm

25 Match each solid to the shapes of its faces. Some have more than one kind.

triangle face   rectangle face   circle face

26 Write the number of corners each shape has.

☐   ☐   ☐   ☐   ☐

27 a Draw a circle in a square above the telephone.

  b Draw a triangle in a square next to the telephone.

  c Draw a cross in a corner square of the grid.

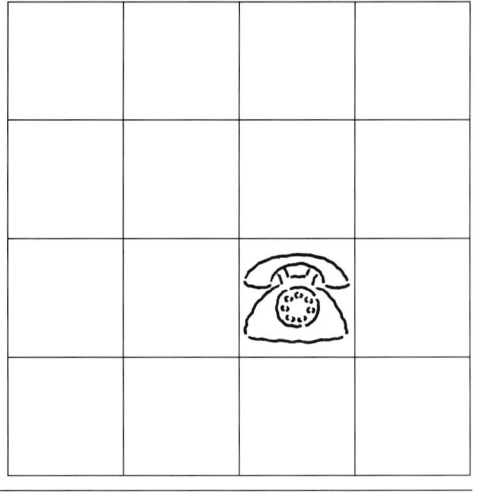

28 These are Peter's instructions to move the counter in the grid.

up 3 squares

right 2 squares

down 1 square

left 3 squares

Draw where the counter will end.

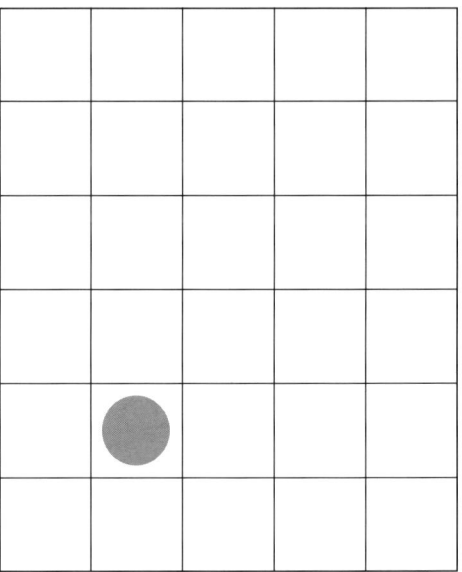

29 Write in the fraction of a whole turn that each strip has made.

a ☐ turn

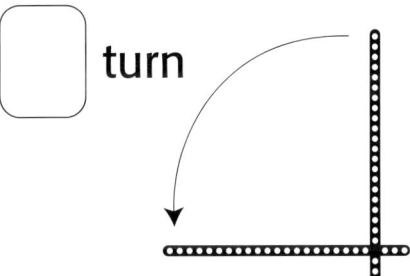

b ☐ turn

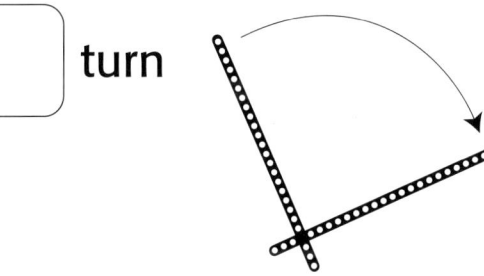

c ☐ turn

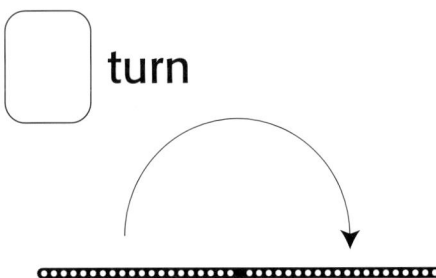

d ☐ turn

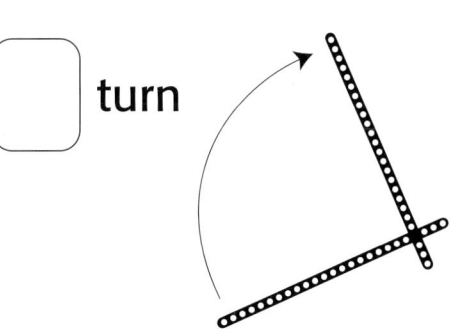

Name:

Date:

Part B

Score out of 101

1

Tick (✓) the **fourth** bus waiting at the bus stop.

2 Imran paid **between 70p and 80p** for the chocolate.

How much do you think he paid? p

3 The number line is marked in **tens**.

0   100

Write where the numbers 40 and 70 go.

4 This is part of a 1 to 100 number square.

Write in the missing numbers.

		17
25		28

5 Match each addition to its answer.

11 + 11	17 + 3	35 + 35	20 + 50	10 + 10

20   22   70

6 Sort the numbers in the oval in the sorting grid.

28 41
19   92
55 76

A multiple of 2	Not a multiple of 2

7 Find the answers.

a

b

c

d

8 The full jar holds **100** sweets.

Estimate the number of
sweets in the other jar. ☐

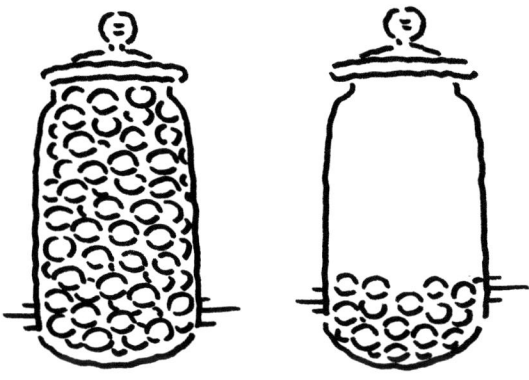

9 a $7 + 6 =$ ☐

b $30 + 59 =$ ☐

c $37 + 10 =$ ☐

d $40 + 50 =$ ☐

10 This is a 0 to 10 number line.

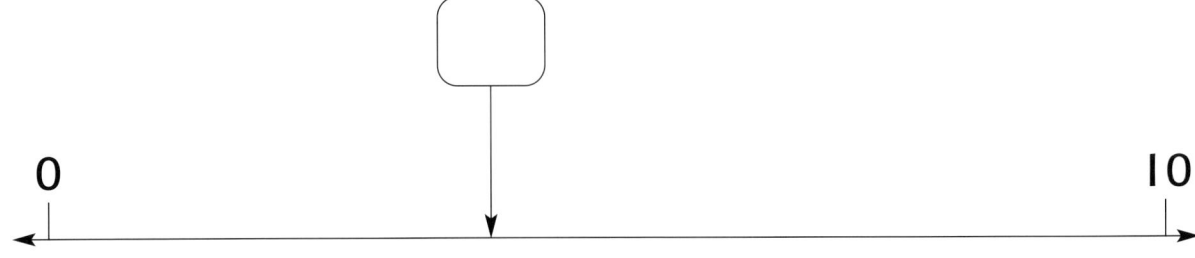

Estimate the whole number marked by the arrow.

11 Circle each number that is a **multiple of 5**.

5   51   20   75   59   40

12 a 60 – 11 = ☐   **b** 35 – 19 = ☐

c 91 – 89 = ☐   **d** 38 – 4 = ☐

13 James pays 35p for an ice cream.

Tick (✓) the coins he could use to pay exactly 35p.

14 a 34 add 10 is ☐   **b** 20 plus 50 is ☐

c What is the total of 3, 12 and 7? ☐

15 a Circle one-half of the eggs.

b What fraction of the large triangle is shaded? ☐

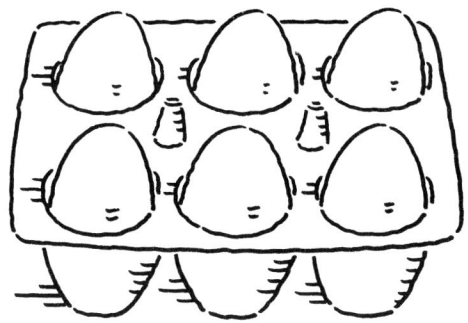

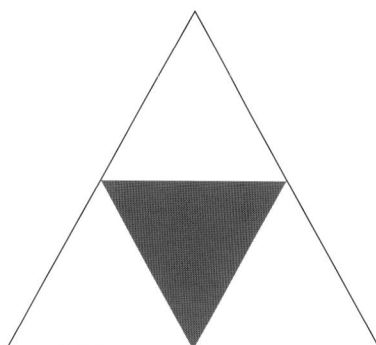

16 a 9 take away 4 equals ⬜

b 17 subtract 3 is ⬜

c How many less is 6 than 15? ⬜

---

17 a $47 + 19 =$ ⬜   **b** $57 + 21 =$ ⬜

c $42 + 5 =$ ⬜   **d** $400 + 300 =$ ⬜

---

18 Write in the missing numbers.

a ⬜ 47 to the nearest ten is ⬜

b ⬜ 93 to the nearest ten is ⬜

c ⬜ to the nearest ten is ⬜ 60

---

19 a $48 - 16 =$ ⬜   **b** $82 - 10 =$ ⬜

---

20 The **total** of each pair of numbers in a row or column is written in a circle.

Put each of the numbers

⬜ 4   ⬜ 2   ⬜ 10   ⬜ 8

in a square so that the totals are correct.

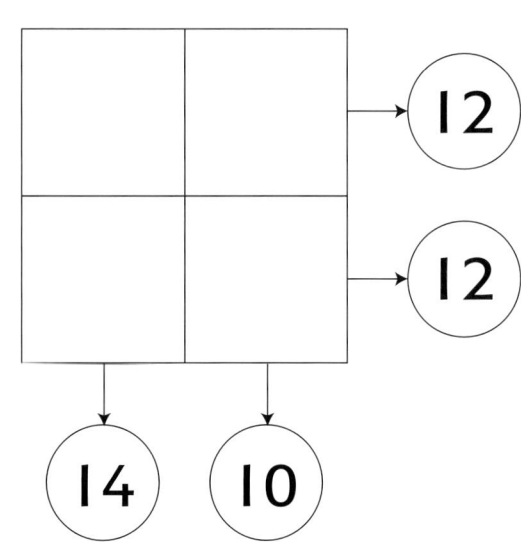

21 a 30 + ☐ = 100   **b** 53 + ☐ = 73

c ☐ + 8 = 13   **d** ☐ + 6 = 25

22

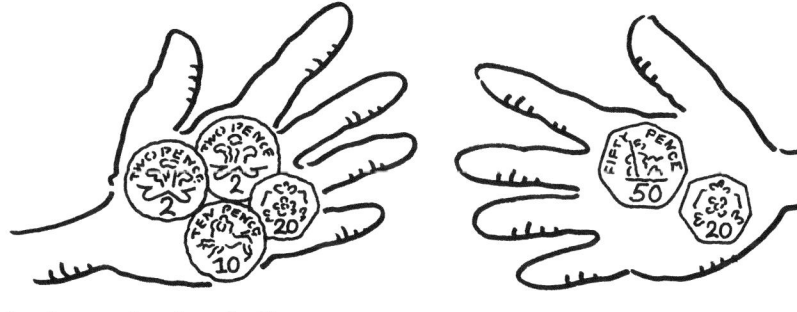

Tick (✓) the hand that is holding 70p.

23 a 60 – ☐ = 10   **b** 47 – ☐ = 27

c 500 – 200 = ☐   **d** ☐ – 9 = 7

e 70 – ☐ = 63   **f** ☐ – 6 = 18

24 Sanjit says, *"There are two numbers between 20 and 25 that divide exactly by 2."*

What are the two numbers? ☐ and ☐

25 Here are two number patterns.

Write in the next two rows in each pattern.

2	+	7	=	9		7	–	2	=	5
2	+	17	=	19		17	–	2	=	15
2	+	27	=	29		27	–	2	=	25
☐	+	☐	=	☐		☐	–	☐	=	☐
☐	+	☐	=	☐		☐	–	☐	=	☐

26 a 200 + ☐ = 206   **b** 50 + ☐ = 67

27 Four children can sit at a table.

How many children altogether can sit at three tables? ☐

28 This is a 0 to 10 number line.

☐

0   1   2   3   4   5   6   7   8   9   10

Write the number marked with the arrow.

29 This is a graph of colour of eyes in Class 2.

Colour of eyes   ⊙ = 1 child

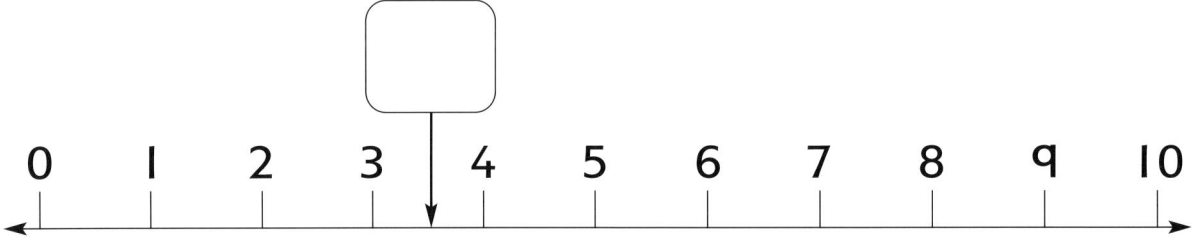

a How many children have green eyes? ☐

b How many more children have blue eyes than have brown eyes? ☐

c How many children are there in Class 2 altogether? ☐

30 Here are three numbers. $\boxed{15}$ $\boxed{18}$ $\boxed{33}$

Use all three numbers each time to complete these additions and subtractions.

$\boxed{15} + \boxed{18} = \boxed{33}$

$\boxed{18} + \boxed{} = \boxed{}$

$\boxed{} - \boxed{} = \boxed{}$

$\boxed{} - \boxed{} = \boxed{}$

31 a $7 \times \boxed{} = 14$ **b** $\boxed{} \times 3 = 30$

c $20 \div 5 = \boxed{}$ **d** $10 \div 2 = \boxed{}$

e Double $8 = \boxed{}$ **f** Half of $26 = \boxed{}$

32 Tina got on the train at 11:30.

She got off the train 2 hours later.

Draw the time on the clock when she got off the train.

33 Match each digital clock to **two** correct times.

quarter past 3		quarter to 3

15 minutes to 3		15 minutes past 3

34 Draw an extra square on each shape. All three shapes must then be different.

35

What is the total cost of one adult ticket and two children's tickets?   £ ⬜

Name: ....

Year 2

Year 2 key objectives	Oral		A		B		C	
	Date	Code	Date	Code	Date	Code	Date	Code
				Written				
1 Count, read, write and order whole numbers to at least 100; know what each digit represents (including 0 as a place holder).								
2 Describe and extend simple number sequences (including odd/even numbers, counting on or back in ones or tens from any 2-digit number, and so on).								
3 Understand that subtraction is the inverse of addition; state the subtraction corresponding to a given addition and vice versa.								
4 Know by heart all addition and subtraction facts for each number to at least 10.								
5 Use knowledge that addition can be done in any order to do mental calculations more efficiently.								
6 Understand the operation of multiplication as repeated addition or as describing an array.								
7 Know and use halving as the inverse of doubling.								
8 Know by heart facts for the 2 and 10 multiplication tables.								
9 Estimate, measure and compare lengths, masses and capacities, using standard units; suggest suitable units and equipment for such measurements.								
10 Read a simple scale to the nearest labelled division, including using a ruler to draw and measure lines to the nearest centimetre.								
11 Use the mathematical names for common 2D and 3D shapes; sort shapes and describe some of their features.								
12 Use mathematical vocabulary to describe position, direction and movement.								
13 Choose and use appropriate operations and efficient calculation strategies to solve problems, explaining how the problem was solved.								

Supplementary notes

Class record sheet

School year

Class ....

NAMES

Year 2 key objectives

1   Count, read, write and order whole numbers to at least 100; know what each digit represents (including 0 as a place holder).

2   Describe and extend simple number sequences (including odd/even numbers, counting on or back in ones or tens from any 2-digit number, and so on).

3   Understand that subtraction is the inverse of addition; state the subtraction corresponding to a given addition and vice versa.

4   Know by heart all addition and subtraction facts for each number to at least 10.

5   Use knowledge that addition can be done in any order to do mental calculations more efficiently.

6   Understand the operation of multiplication as repeated addition or as describing an array.

7   Know and use halving as the inverse of doubling.

8   Know by heart facts for the 2 and 10 multiplication tables.

9   Estimate, measure and compare lengths, masses and capacities, using standard units; suggest suitable units and equipment for such measurements.

10   Read a simple scale to the nearest labelled division, including using a ruler to draw and measure lines to the nearest centimetre.

11   Use the mathematical names for common 2D and 3D shapes; sort shapes and describe some of their features.

12   Use mathematical vocabulary to describe position, direction and movement.

13   Choose and use appropriate operations and efficient calculation strategies to solve problems, explaining how the problem was solved.

Getting ready: Part A

Getting ready: Part B

National Curriculum Levels record sheet

	Name	Raw score	Working towards Level 1			Level 1			Level 2			Level 3	Level 4
			Percentage score										
			0	10	20	30	40	50	60	70	80	90	100
1													
2													
3													
4													
5													
6													
7													
8													
9													
10													
11													
12													
13													
14													
15													
16													
17													
18													
19													
20													
21													
22													
23													
24													
25													
26													
27													
28													
29													
30													
31													
32													
33													
34													
36													
36													

Answers

Written assessment 1A

1   47

2

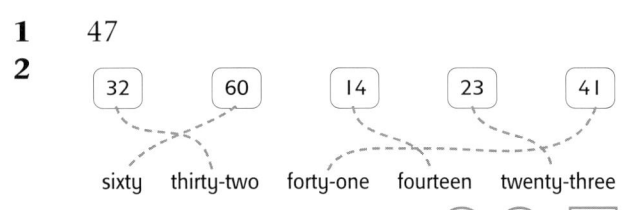

32   60   14   23   41

sixty   thirty-two   forty-one   fourteen   twenty-three

3   92, 54, 45, 30, 29   **4**   (29) (20) [37]

Written assessment 1B

1   37   **2**   26   **3**   78
4   nineteen, 43, ninety-four, 80
5   7, 12 , 21, 50, 78, 87
6   38, 5, 27, 60
7

| 0 | | 30 | 50 | | 80 | 100 |

8   5 tens 4 ones,
     8 tens 0 ones,
     0 tens 7 ones,
     6 tens 1 one

Written assessment 1C

1   34

2

		77	78
	86	87	88
	96	97	

3a   24, 42, 74, 27, 72
 b   72
 c   any five of 74, 72, 47, 42, 27, 24 in
      order

Written assessment 2A

1   16 to 21 inclusive
2   24 to 19 inclusive
3   41, 51, 61, 71, 81, 91
4   56, 46, 36, 26, 16, 6
5   2, 4, 6, 8, 10, 12, 14

Written assessment 2B

1   42, 43, 44, ..., 48, 49, 50, 51

2   61, 60, 59, ..., 55, 54, 53, 52
3   3, 13, 23, ..., 63, 73, 83, 93
4   96, 86, 76, ..., 36, 26, 16, 6
5   7, 23, 35   **6**   10, 24, 30, 32
7a   52   **b**   26
 c   4   **d**   5
8a   54   **b**   25
 c   4 tens or 40   **d**   3 tens or 30

Written assessment 2C

1   28, 29, 39   **2**   odd numbers:
     29, 39, 38   29, 11, 43, 65
     59, 60, 50   even numbers:
     49, 39, 38   52, 70, 38, 94
3   66, 76, 86
     31, 29, 27
     24, 26, 28

Written assessment 3A

1a   1, 5   **b**   10, 30   **c**   2, 12
2a   9, 6   **b**   40, 20   **c**   24, 14
3a   5 − 3 = 2 or 5 − 2 = 3
 b   40 − 10 = 30 or 40 − 30 = 10
4a   4 + 2 = 6 or 2 + 4 = 6
 b   10 + 20 = 30 or 20 + 10 = 30

Written assessment 3B

1a   22, 6   **b**   90, 50   **c**   45, 35
 d   e.g. + and − undo each other
2a   12, 17   **b**   40, 70   **c**   39, 49
 d   e.g. − and + are inverse operations
3a   25 − 8 = 17 or 25 − 17 = 8
 b   80 − 50 = 30 or 80 − 30 = 50
4a   6 + 13 = 19 or 13 + 6 = 19
 b   50 + 20 = 70 or 20 + 50 = 70
5a   42   **b**   20   **c**   32
 d   30   **e**   55   **f**   400
6a   95   **b**   60   **c**   36
 d   54   **e**   80   **f**   600
7   24 + 31 = 55   31 + 24 = 55
     55 − 24 = 31   55 − 31 = 24

Written assessment 3C

1a	71, 80	**b**	66, 66	**c**	97, 57
2a	78, 50	**b**	67, 67	**c**	500, 800
3a	79	**b**	30		
4a	16	**b**	97		

5a e.g. 83 − 2 + 2 = 83
  b e.g. 83 − 70 + 70 = 83
  c e.g. 83 − 29 + 29 = 83

Written assessment 4A

1 4, 7

2

+	1	2	3	4	5
1	2	3	4	5	6
2	3	4	5	6	7
3	4	5	6	7	8
4	5	6	7	8	9
5	6	7	8	9	10

−	1	2	3	4	5
6	5	4	3	2	1
7	6	5	4	3	2
8	7	6	5	4	3
9	8	7	6	5	4
10	9	8	7	6	5

3a	5	**b**	5	**c**	4
d	6	**e**	7	**f**	6
4a	2	**b**	2	**c**	0
d	3	**e**	1	**f**	1

Written assessment 4B

1a

+	2	6	4
3	5	9	7
1	3	7	5
4	6	10	8

b

+	1	4	3
6	7	10	9
2	3	6	5
5	6	9	8

2a

−	3	0	1
6	3	6	5
9	6	9	8
4	1	4	3

b

−	2	5	4
7	5	2	3
5	3	0	1
8	6	3	4

3a	9	**b**	7	**c**	5
d	10	**e**	6	**f**	8
g	9	**h**	5	**i**	10
4a	3	**b**	6	**c**	0
d	2	**e**	2	**f**	4
g	2	**h**	1	**i**	7

5

number	2	0	5	3	2	8	4	5	7	0
number	8	7	2	0	6	1	3	5	2	10
sum	10	7	7	3	8	9	7	10	9	10

6

number	2	10	5	9	4	10	3	8	9	7
number	0	3	1	4	2	6	2	3	9	6
difference	2	7	4	5	2	4	1	5	0	1

7a	open	**b**	open
c	open	**d**	open
8a	open	**b**	open

c	open	**d**	open
9a	9	**b**	7
c	3	**d**	10

Written assessment 4C

1a

+	5	1	6
3	8	4	9
0	5	1	6
4	9	5	10

b

−	5	0	3
9	4	9	6
5	0	5	2
10	5	10	7

2a

number	2	6	9	3
number	7	2	0	7
sum	9	8	9	10

b

number	6	7	8 or 10	8
number	10 or 2	7	9	9 or 7
difference	4	0	1	1

3a	3	**b**	2	**c**	2
d	4	**4**	open		

Written assessment 5A

1a	21	**b**	21	**c**	22	**d**	22
2a	60	**b**	60	**c**	40	**d**	40
3a	15	**b**	15	**c**	14	**d**	14

4 25 and child's explanation
5 16 and child's explanation

Written assessment 5B

1 33 and child's explanation
2 120 and child's explanation
3 57 and child's explanation
4 406 and child's explanation
5 47 and child's explanation
6 52 and child's explanation
7 59 and child's explanation
8 900 and child's explanation
9 19 and child's explanation

Written assessment 5C

1a	39	**b**	7
2a	50	**b**	8
3a	500	**b**	9
4a	60	**b**	80
5a	41	**b**	73
6a	62	**b**	10
7a	60	**b**	60
8a	60	**b**	80
9a	62	**b**	20
10a	5	**b**	9

Written assessment 6A

1a 2 **b** 6 **c** 6 **d** 6
2a 4 **b** 3 **c** 12 **d** 12
 e 12 **f** 12 **g** 12
3a 15 **b** 15 **c** 15

Written assessment 6B

1a 4 **b** 2 **c** 8
 d 8 **e** 8
2a 3 **b** 5 **c** 15
 d 15 **e** 15 **f** 15
 g 15
3a 12 **b** 12 **c** 12
 d 12
4a 5, 20 **b** 3, 18 **c** 5, 2, 10
5a

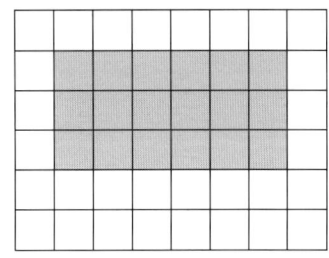

or similar
 b 18
6a 3, 21 **b** 6, 24 **c** 5, 8, 40

Written assessment 6C

1a 2, 2, 2, 6 **b** 3, 18
 c 3, 15 **d** 5, 4, 20
2a 4, 24 **b** 5, 40
 c 10, 3, 30
3a 4, 28 **b** 4, 20
 c 2, 8, 16
4a 5, 30 **b** 7, 21
 c 2, 9, 18

Written assessment 7A

1a 5 **b** 10
2a 8 **b** 4
3 2, 1 4, 2 6, 3 8, 4
4 5, 10 4, 8 3, 6 2, 4

Written assessment 7B

1a 24, 12 **b** 10, 20
2

halve	3	7	2	5	15	9	10	25
number	6	14	4	10	30	18	20	50
double	12	28	8	20	60	36	40	100

3 26, 13 50, 25 18, 9   90, 45 70, 35
4 8, 16 30, 60 11, 22 35, 70 45, 90
5a 17 **b** 60
 c 22 **d** 100
6a 38 **b** 70
 c 46 **d** 300

Written assessment 7C

1 8, 8   35, 70
2 14, 14   50, 25
3

halve	6	20	2	7	15	9	$22\frac{1}{2}$	150
number	12	40	4	14	30	18	45	300
double	24	80	8	28	60	36	90	600

4 8, 16   open
5 32, 32   open

Written assessment 8A

1 8 **2** 50 **3** 70
4a 2 **b** 8 **c** 4
 d 6
5a 10 **b** 30 **c** 40
 d 20

Written assessment 8B

1a

×	2	10
4	8	40
7	14	70
3	6	30
1	2	10
5	10	50

b

×	2	10
10	20	100
2	4	20
9	18	90
8	16	80
6	12	60

2a 10 **b** 2 **c** 16
 d 6 **e** 18 **f** 8
 g 14 **h** 4 **i** 12
3a 50 **b** 90 **c** 60
 d 20 **e** 80 **f** 30
4a 6 **b** 40 **c** 12
 d 70
5 6 **6** 30
7a 10 **b** 12 **c** 16
 d 6 **e** 18 **f** 8
 g 14 **h** 20
8a 70 **b** 90 **c** 60
 d 40 **e** 80 **f** 30

Written assessment 8C

1

×	3	9	4	1
2	6	18	8	2
10	30	90	40	10

×	8	2	5	6
10	80	20	50	60
2	16	4	10	12

2a 2   **b** 2   **c** 6
 d 7   **e** 10   **f** 2
3a 7   **b** 10   **c** 10
 d 6   **e** 9   **f** 5
4a twos   **b** 7   **c** ten
 d 3

Written assessment 9A

1

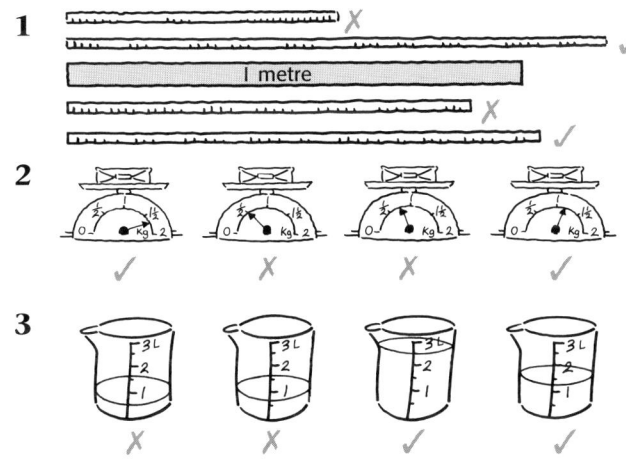

2

3

Written assessment 9B

1a 80, 90, 65   **b** Mara   **c** Bruce
2a 7, 10, 8
 b, c

3 8   **4** 5, 6 or 7
5 cat or ladybird   **6** lorry
7 bucket
8a metres   **b** litres
 c kilograms

Written assessment 9C

1a 20   **b** 5
2a 12   **b** 3
3a 8   **b** 2

Written assessment 10A

1 4, 6, 5   **2** 2, 7, 4   **3** 3, 6, 1

Written assessment 10B

1a 10   **b** 6   **c** 9
2a 7   **b** 4
3a 7   **b** 9
4a 1   **b** 4   **c** 3
5a 3   **b** 1   **c** 5
6a $4\frac{1}{2}$ **b** $5\frac{1}{2}$ **c** $8\frac{1}{2}$

Written assessment 10C

1a 1   **b** 11   **c** 2
2a 8   **b** $7\frac{1}{2}$
3   **4**

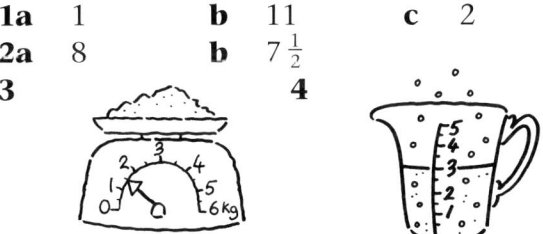

Written assessment 11A

1

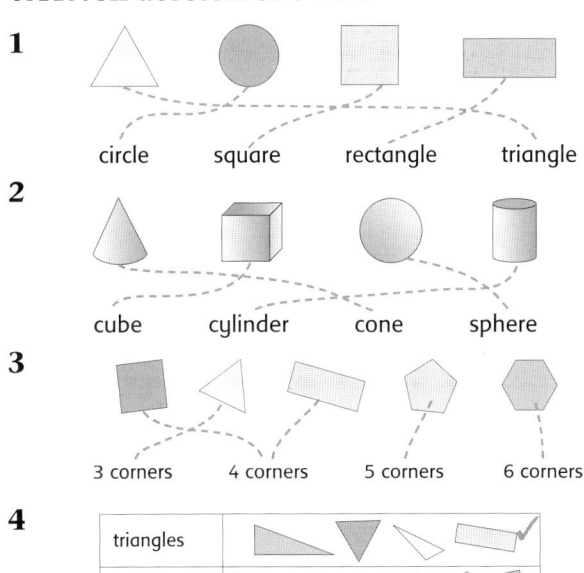

2

3

4

triangles	
rectangles	

Written assessment 11B

1

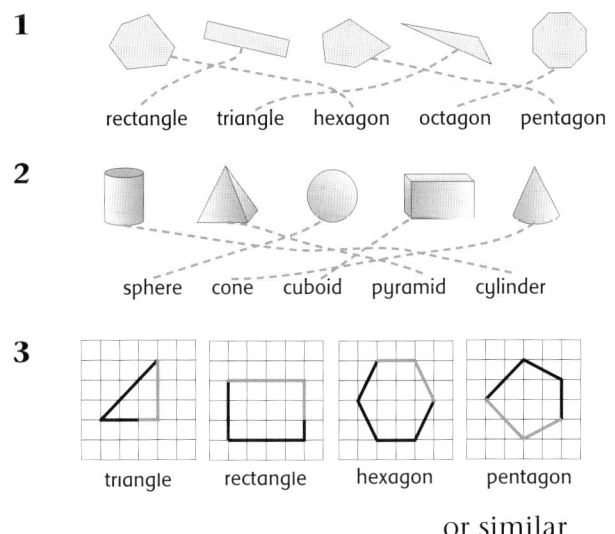

2

3

triangle   rectangle   hexagon   pentagon

or similar

4

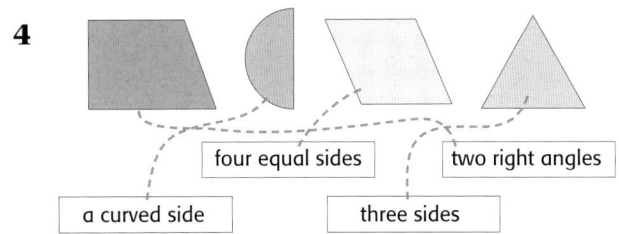

four equal sides
two right angles
a curved side
three sides

5

	number of flat faces	number of curved faces	number of edges
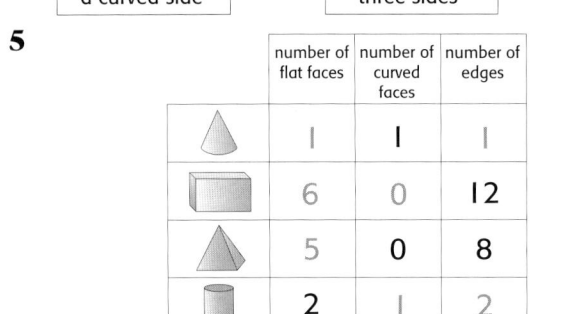	1	1	1
	6	0	12
	5	0	8
	2	1	2

6

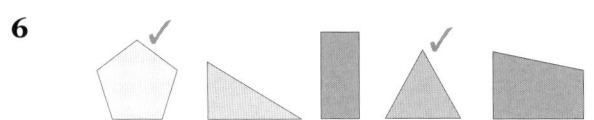

Written assessment 11C

1

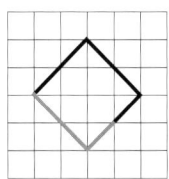 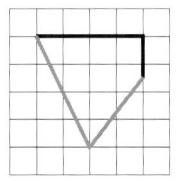

or similar

2

	number of flat faces	number of corners	number of edges
a triangular prism	4	6	9
a hemisphere	1	0	1
a square pyramid	5	5	8

3

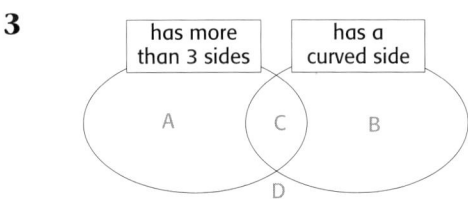

has more than 3 sides   has a curved side

A   C   B

D

Written assessment 12A

1   **2**

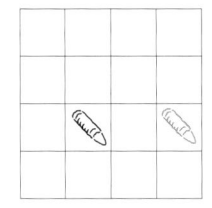

or similar

3

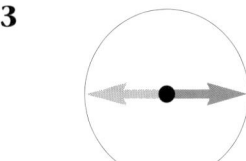

Written assessment 12B

1   left 2   up 1   left 1
2a   next   **b**   above   **c**   edge
 d   right
3   **a**   **b**   **c**

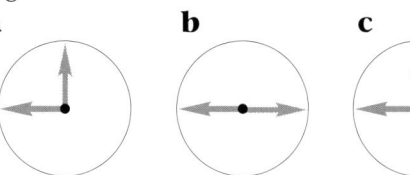

4

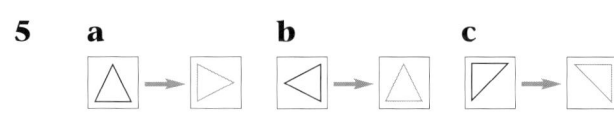

5   **a**   **b**   **c**

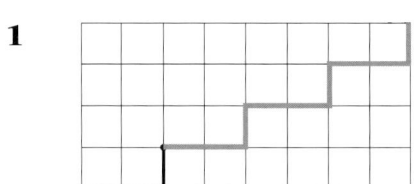

Written assessment 12C

1

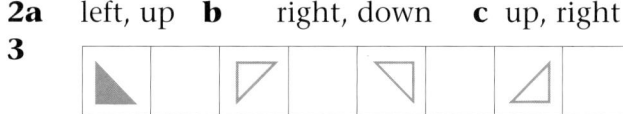

2a   left, up   **b**   right, down   **c**   up, right
3

Written assessment 13A

1a   –   **b**   +   **c**   –
2   child's own story
3   9 and child's explanation

Written assessment 13B

1a   –   **b**   +   **c**   ×
2   child's own story
3   child's own story
4a   –, +   **b**   ×, +
5   17 and child's explanation
6   53 and child's explanation
7   30 and child's explanation

Written assessment 13C

1a   +, =, –   **b**   ×, –, = or ×, =, +
 c   –, =, ×
2   child's own story
3   50 and child's explanation

Getting ready Part A

1a 14 (1m) **b** 40 (1m)

2a

		25	26	27	28				32

(1m)

b 6 tens or 60 (1m)

3

3	6	9
12	15	18
21	24	27
30	33	36

(6m)

4 18, 16, 14, 12 (4m)

5 5, …, 30, …, 50 (3m)

6 eighteen, 73, thirty-seven, 81 (4m)

7 four 10p and three 1p (1m)

8a 80 (1m) **b** 9 (1m) **c** open (1m)

9 91, 63, 36, 19 (4m)

10 50, 30 (2m) 57, 60 (2m)
child's explanation (1m)

11a

+	3	8	5
2	5	10	7
7	10	15	12
5	8	13	10

b

–	4	1	6
9	5	8	3
7	3	6	1
10	6	9	4

(9 m) (9 m)

12a 27, 36 (2m) **b** 50, 80 (2m)

13 10, 30 (2m) 2, 8 (2m)

14 2 (1m)

15 10, 5 (2m) 10, 20 (2m)
child's explanation (1m)

16a

×	3	5	2	4
2	6	10	4	8
10	30	50	20	40

b

×	8	7	9	6
10	80	70	90	60
2	16	14	18	12

(8m) (8m)

17 child's own story (1m)

18 –, ×, + (3m)

19

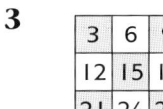

(4m)

20

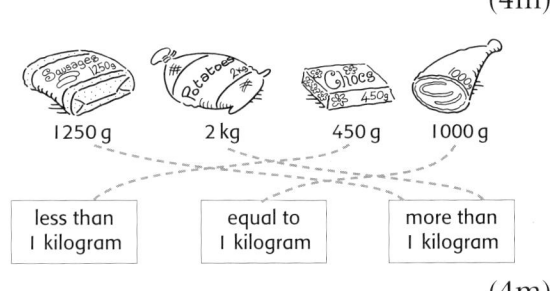

1250 g   2 kg   450 g   1000 g

less than 1 kilogram   equal to 1 kilogram   more than 1 kilogram

(4m)

21

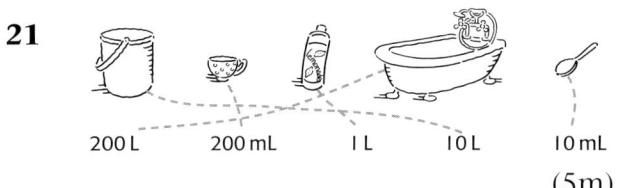

200 L   200 mL   1 L   10 L   10 mL

(5m)

22 55, 70, 20 (3m)

23 4, 2, (2m)

24 A to B =14, B to C = 5, C to D = 7, D to A = 9 (4m)

25

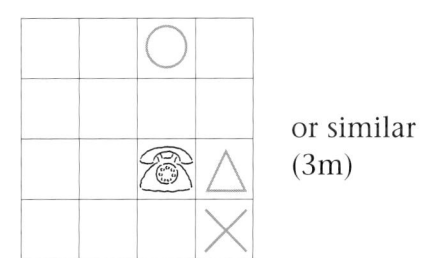

triangle face   rectangle face   circle face

(7m)

26 4, 4, 5, 3, 6 (5m)

27a, b, c

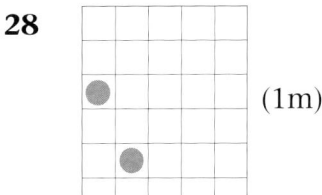

or similar (3m)

28

or similar

(1m)

29a $\frac{1}{4}$ (1m) **b** $\frac{1}{4}$ (1m)
c $\frac{1}{2}$ (1m) **d** $\frac{1}{4}$ (1m)

Getting ready Part B

1

(1m)

2 75 (1m)

3

0		40	70	100

(2m)

4

	17		
25	26	27	28
35		37	

(4m)

5

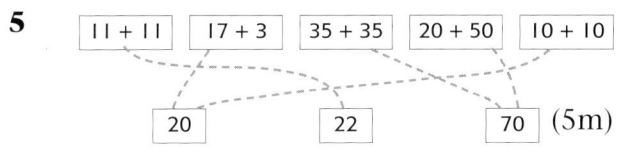

11 + 11   17 + 3   35 + 35   20 + 50   10 + 10

20   22   70   (5m)

95

6

A multiple of 2			Not a multiple of 2		
28	92	76	19	41	55

(6m)

7a 50 (1m)   **b** 69 (1m)
  c 25 (1m)   **d** 80 (1m)
8 20 to 30 inclusive (1m)
9a 13 (1m)   **b** 89 (1m)
  c 47 (1m)   **d** 90 (1m)
10 4 (1m)
11 5, 20, 75, 40 (4m)
12a 49 (1m)   **b** 16 (1m)
  c 2 (1m)   **d** 34 (1m)
13 one 20p, one 10p, one 5p (1m)
14a 44 (1m)   **b** 70 (1m)   **c** 22 (1m)
15a 3 (1m)   **b** $\frac{1}{4}$ (1m)
16a 5 (1m)   **b** 14 (1m)   **c** 9 (1m)
17a 66 (1m)   **b** 78 (1m)
  c 47 (1m)   **d** 700 (1m)
18a 50 (1m)   **b** 90 (1m)
  c 55 to 64 inclusive (1m)
19a 32 (1m)   **b** 72 (1m)
20

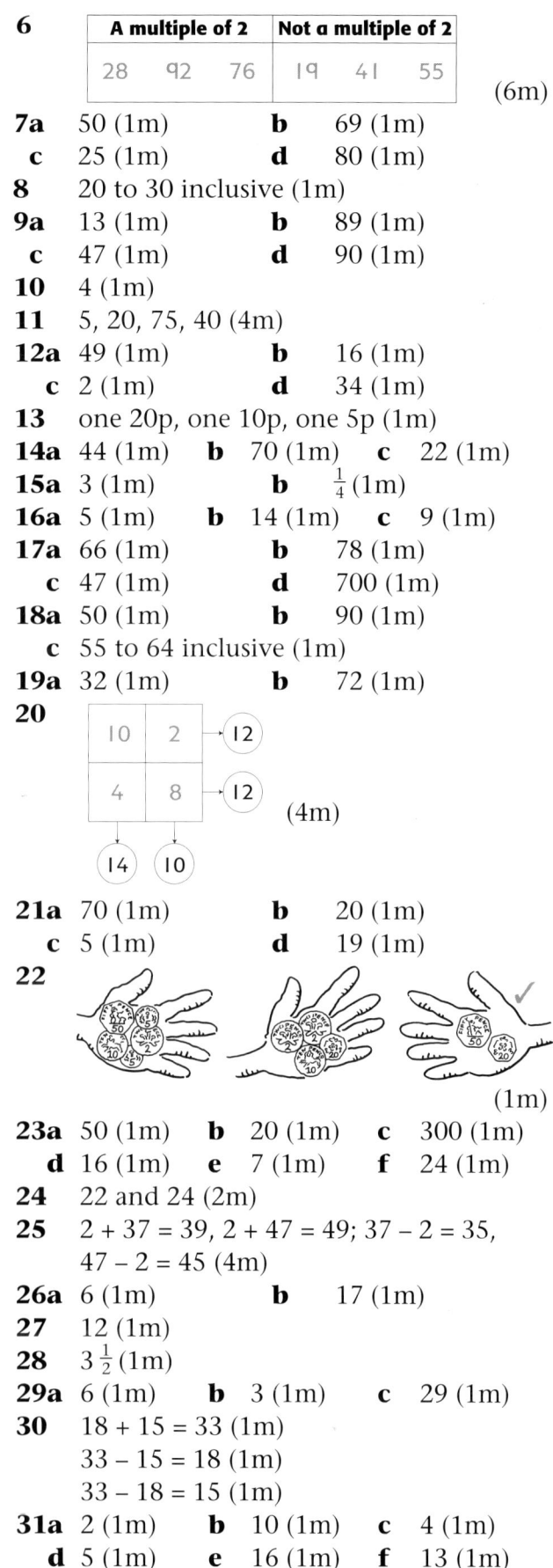

(4m)

21a 70 (1m)   **b** 20 (1m)
  c 5 (1m)   **d** 19 (1m)
22

(1m)

23a 50 (1m)   **b** 20 (1m)   **c** 300 (1m)
  d 16 (1m)   **e** 7 (1m)   **f** 24 (1m)
24 22 and 24 (2m)
25 2 + 37 = 39, 2 + 47 = 49; 37 – 2 = 35,
  47 – 2 = 45 (4m)
26a 6 (1m)   **b** 17 (1m)
27 12 (1m)
28 $3\frac{1}{2}$ (1m)
29a 6 (1m)   **b** 3 (1m)   **c** 29 (1m)
30 18 + 15 = 33 (1m)
  33 – 15 = 18 (1m)
  33 – 18 = 15 (1m)
31a 2 (1m)   **b** 10 (1m)   **c** 4 (1m)
  d 5 (1m)   **e** 16 (1m)   **f** 13 (1m)

32

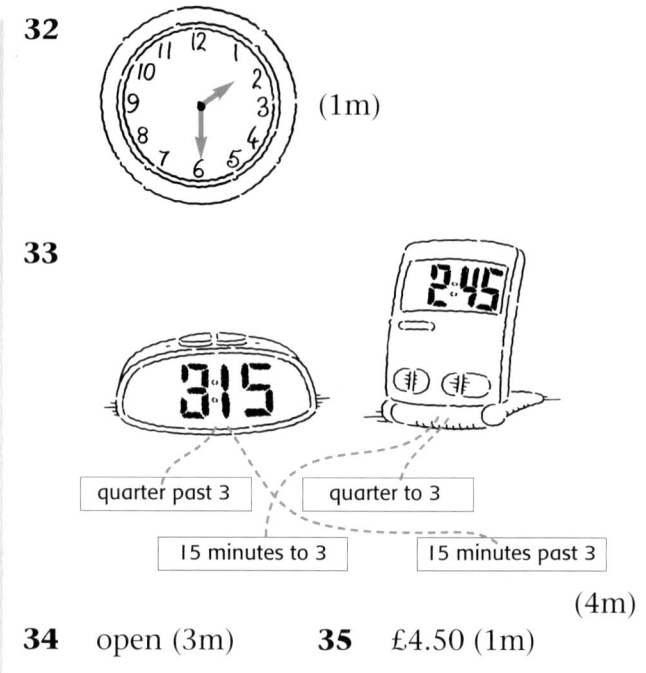

(1m)

33

| quarter past 3 | quarter to 3 |
| 15 minutes to 3 | 15 minutes past 3 |

(4m)

34 open (3m)   **35** £4.50 (1m)

The total number of marks for Getting ready
Part A is 128.
The total number of marks for Getting ready
Part B is 101.
Final total for the whole of the Getting ready
test = 128 + 101 = 229.
'open' means there are many alternative
answers.
The number in the brackets (e.g. 4m) after
each answer is the number of marks awarded
to that question or part question.